Fearfully & WONDERFULLY Created

By

Renele Awono

© 2019 by Renele Awono
Fearfully and Wonderfully Created

All rights reserved. No portion of this book may be reproduced, stored in a retrieval system, or transmitted in any form or by means-electronic, mechanical, photocopy, recording, scanning, or other-except for brief quotations in critical reviews or articles, without prior permission of the publisher.

Published in Fontana, California by Altar Books. Altar Books is a registered trademark of Quiver Full Publishing, Inc.

Altar Books titles may be purchased in bulk for educational, business, fundraising, or sales promotional use. For information, please e-mail *yvonnedcamper@gmail.com*

Unless otherwise noted, Scriptures used in this volume are taken from the Holy Bible, the New King James Version®. Copyright © 1982 by Thomas Nelson. Used by permission. All rights reserved.

Scripture quotations designated ESV are from The Holy Bible, English Standard Version ®, copyright © 2001 by Crossway Bibles, a publishing ministry of Good News Publishers. Used by permission. All rights reserved.

Scriptures noted (NIV) are taken from the Holy Bible, New International Version®, NIV® Copyright ©1973, 1978, 1984, 2011 by Biblica, Inc.® Used by permission. All rights reserved worldwide.

Scripture taken from the New King James Version®. Copyright © 1982 by Thomas Nelson, Inc. Used by permission. All rights reserved.

Scriptures noted (MSG) are taken from the Holy Bible, The Message, Copyright © 1993, 1994, 1995, 1996, 2000, 2001, 2002 by Eugene H. Peterson.

Scriptures noted (AMP) are taken from the Holy Bible, Amplified Bible, Copyright © 2015 by The Lockman Foundation, La Habra, CA 90631. All rights reserved.

Scriptures noted (NASB) are taken from the Holy Bible, New American Standard Bible, Copyright © 1960, 1962, 1963, 1968, 1971, 1972, 1973, 1975, 1977, 1995 by The Lockman Foundation.

Scriptures noted (NLT) are taken from the Holy Bible, New Living Translation, copyright © 1996, 2004, 2015 by Tyndale House Foundation. Used by permission of Tyndale House Publishers Inc., Carol Stream, Illinois 60188. All rights reserved.

Paperback:

ISBN-13: 978-1-7325276-2-1

Library of Congress Control Number:

Printed in the United States of America

DEDICATIONS

To God who gave me Ps. 139:14 as a personal theme long before I even understood it fully. To my beloved husband, Yves, who constantly prayed for me to have God's inspiration to write, to my amazing children that have always encouraged me to be adventurous from writing books to traveling around the world. To my mom, who has continued to pray for me throughout the years. To my awesome friends Dawn Bracken & Taniysha Mebane who have walked with me through life and alongside of me during the penning of this book. To Yvonne Camper who has truly been a midwife, helping me to bring into this earth what God placed on the inside of me. Thank you for the wisdom, motivation and transformation God has allowed you to bring into my life, it has been priceless. Thank you all for your love and support!

FOREWORD

Fearfully and Wonderfully Created is a compelling read that reminds us all that God crafted an exquisite masterpiece when He created mankind. The compelling argument is there is a divine design for your life, and it is not just a random act. This book will help you understand why you are here, how do you find purpose? and what to do once you find it?

Even for the most seasoned believers, this book is a wonderful refresher that we are not just taking up space but there is a masterplan in place by a master builder. It is a must read for anyone contemplating purpose, destiny, and fulfillment in life.

The three pinnacles of thought the author has painted are, laying the foundation, overcoming obstacles and the journey. These pillars help the reader not only glean from the author but implement what they have learned. I encourage you to read this book and learn from the best. Destiny awaits you!

Yvonne Camper
Founder of Yvonne Camper Ministries
Author, Speaker, Mentor, Leader

INTRODUCTION

Fearfully and Wonderfully Created is based upon Psalms 139:14 Amplified version which says, "I will give thanks, and praise to you for I am fearfully and wonderfully made; wonderful are your works, and my soul knows it very well. David pauses amid his writing to give God praise for creating him and uses the most distinctive choice of words to describe how well God made him. The word fearfully here means, "set apart and unique." James Orr defines "wonder" in the Old Testament as a "miraculous work, that which excites or calls forth wonder so in the New Testament the feeling of wonder is chiefly drawn out by marvelous displays of Christ's power & wisdom."[1] It is both powerful and humbling to know that we are fearfully & wonderfully made through the power & wisdom of God!

The story of Creation also gives us insight into how God created everything out of absolutely nothing. Take a moment to read it below Genesis 1 Message Bible:

Day One
1-2 First this: God created the Heavens and Earth—all you see, all you don't see. Earth was a soup of nothingness, a bottomless emptiness, an inky blackness. God's Spirit brooded like a bird above the watery abyss. 3-5 God spoke: "Light!" and light appeared. God saw that light was good and separated light from dark. God named the light Day, he named the dark Night. It was evening, it was morning—

Day Two
6-8 God spoke: "Sky! In the middle of the waters; separate water from the water!" God made the sky. He separated the water under the sky from the water above the sky. And there it was: he named sky the Heavens; It was evening, it was morning—

Day Three

9-10 God spoke: "Separate! Water-beneath-Heaven, gather into one place; Land, appear!" And there it was. God named the land Earth. He named the pooled water Ocean. God saw that it was good. 11-13 God spoke: "Earth, green up! Grow all varieties of seed-bearing plants, Every sort of fruit-bearing tree." And there it was. Earth produced green seed-bearing plants, all varieties, And fruit-bearing trees of all sorts. God saw that it was good. It was evening, it was morning—

Day Four

14-15 God spoke: "Lights! Come out! Shine in Heaven's sky! Separate Day from Night. Mark seasons and days and years, Lights in Heaven's sky to give light to Earth." And there it was. 16-19 God made two big lights, the larger to take charge of Day, The smaller to be in charge of Night, and he made the stars. God placed them in the heavenly sky to light up Earth And oversee Day and Night, to separate light and dark. God saw that it was good. It was evening, it was morning—

Day Five

20-23 God spoke: "Swarm, Ocean, with fish and all sea life! Birds, fly through the sky over Earth!" God created the huge whales, all the swarm of life in the waters, And every kind and species of flying birds. God saw that it was good. God blessed them: "Prosper! Reproduce! Fill Ocean! Birds, reproduce on Earth!" It was evening, it was morning—

Day Six

24-25 God spoke: "Earth, generate life! Every sort and kind: cattle and reptiles and wild animals—all kinds." And there it was: Wild animals of every kind, Cattle of all kinds, every sort of reptile and bug. God saw that it was good. 26-28 God spoke: "Let us make human beings in our image, make them reflecting our nature so they can be responsible for the fish in the sea, the birds in the air, the cattle, And, yes, Earth itself, and every animal that moves on the face of Earth." God created human beings; He created them godlike, Reflecting God's nature. He created them male and female. God blessed them: "Prosper! Reproduce! Fill Earth! Take charge! Be responsible for fish in the sea and birds in *the air, for every living thing that moves on the face of Earth."29-30 Then God said, "I've given you every sort of seed-bearing plant on Earth And every kind of fruit-bearing tree, given them to you for food. To all animals and all birds, everything that moves and breathes, I give whatever grows out of the ground for food." And there it was. 31 God looked over everything he had made; it was so good, so very food! It was evening, it was morning—*

The Bible even describes how "by Him, all things were created, in heaven and on earth, visible and invisible, whether thrones or dominions or rulers or authorities—all things were created through Him and for Him. And He is before all things, and in Him, all things hold together." (Colossians 1: 16-17 ESV) That is amazing in itself; it truly speaks to the fact that God is sovereign and needs no help in doing what He desires to do. After creating all the animals, the universe and the sea God saved the best for last and made us in their image, the image of the Father, Son & Holy Spirit. We are made in the image and likeness of God.

As we explore our creation more closely, we see that we are the most complex unique creatures on earth, which is exciting and sparks curiosity! "What exactly did David see when he described how he was made." He certainly understood something that many of us don't. He was intentionally created with love and purpose by God.

Let's take a journey together into the heart of the matter, why on earth are we here? Many of us have asked this question for far too long, some have even given up. Instead, we live each day with no real sense of purpose. I am not going to pretend to have all the answers to such a complex question with many varying circumstances; however, we can take a journey together that may very well provide a starting point and lead you in the right direction. Again, this book is biblically based and rooted in the story of Creation. If you have never explored the Bible or the Creation, I encourage you to keep reading and promise that you will discover a new perspective on why you are here on this earth. It is my prayer that what you read in this book will not only change how you think about who you are but that it will assist you in completely aligning with your true destiny and purpose in this earth.

xiii

TABLE OF CONTENTS

Part 1 – LAYING THE FOUNDATION OF TRUTH ...1

Chapter 1 THE TRUTH ABOUT GOD ...3

Chapter 2 CHOSEN VS. CREATED ...11

Chapter 3 THE TRUTH ABOUT ME ...19

Chapter 4 CO-CREATING WITH GOD ...29

Part 2 – OVERCOMING OBSTACLES ...37

Chapter 5 NO LONGER AN ORPHAN ...39

Chapter 6 CRUSHING REJCTION ...51

Chapter 7 THE BRIDGE CALLED SURRENDER ...63

Chapter 8 FAKE ID's ...75

Chapter 9 WHAT DO YOU BELIEVE? ...83

Part 3 – THE JOURNEY ...95

Chapter 10 PIECES ...97

Chapter 11 ORDINARY TO EXTRAORDINARY ...109

Chapter 12 HIDDEN IN PLAIN SIGHT...................121

Chapter 13 ENCOURAGEMENT FOR THE WEARY . 129

Chapter 14 A RICH INHERITANCE................................. 139

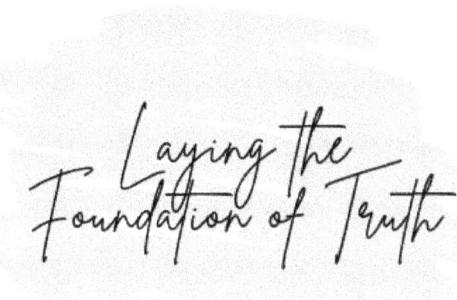

Part 1

This section of the book is crucial to understanding the truth. Everything that you read after this will build on the foundation set in this section. Expert builders have a clear understanding of what they are commissioned to do. Whether constructing a house or a skyscraper, the foundation is the most integral part of the structure. It determines whether the building will remain standing or crumble down. The Bible even discusses how a wise man built his house on the rock and the storms, winds and rain beat on the house and it did not fall because it was founded on the rock, a sure foundation. Conversely, there was a foolish man who built his house on the sand, and when the rains descended, the winds and the floods came to beat down on the house, and it fell. The scriptures add, "and great was its fall" (Matthew 7:24-27 KJV). The rock is Jesus, the Word of God. The Word comes to sure up your foundation, seal up the cracks, the wrong beliefs, and mindsets that keep you from pursuing your purpose and making the impact that God intended.

Chapter 1

THE TRUTH ABOUT GOD

In the beginning, I mean in the very, very beginning, before you were conceived, you were on the heart and mind of God. For some that may be unimaginable and others simply don't believe it. When you see a beautiful painting, an elegant dance performed, watch a movie that tugs at your heartstrings, hold a unique piece of pottery or even look a stunning photo something happens to you on the inside. Most often questions come to mind like, what was the artist thinking? What story was he or she trying to tell? Take for example Michelangelo, "what made him lay on his back for hours to paint the ceiling of the Sistine Chapel?" Without question, we understand that he wanted others to look up and enjoy his uniquely designed masterpiece. So that then begs the questions why were we created, what story was God trying to tell in and through our lives, what did He have in mind when He created us? And for what purpose were we designed?

For us to even begin to understand our significance on earth, we must go back to the beginning. Before God created the earth there was nothing, the earth was without form and void, empty, there was no light (Genesis 1:2 ESV.) In the midst of darkness, He had you in mind and for the next five days took His time to create a place for you to inhabit. It was not until the earth was fully created that He began to make the most intelligent design on earth, you! By day six He began to create man and woman fully knowing that there would be generations that would come after His initial creation. Their creation is significant because it speaks of how valuable and precious you are to God. There was no need for God to create human beings; He created you from a heart of love and intention.

The Creator's Intention

Do you know how much you are known and loved by God? Many of us don't know or fully understand the depths of God's love for us. David described with such passion and confidence just how much God adores us. Let's take a more in-depth look into Psalms 139: 13 & 15 NIV: "For you created my inmost being; you knit me together in my mother's womb." "My frame was not hidden from you when I was made in the secret place when I was woven together in the depths of the earth."

When you create something, a fondness develops for your creation. Think about when you bake a cake or build a piece of furniture, you have an endearing appreciation because time, effort, creativity and strategy went into your work. Though your creation cannot tangibly give you anything in return, you, still have a deep sense of appreciation for it. Imagine the mother that carries her child in her womb for nine months, watches it grow, feels it move and finally gets to touch, hold and interact with what was once a physical part of her. There is such a deep bond between a mother and her child.

The God of the universe took His time to create your innermost being. David, who was often called the Psalmist, describes how nothing was hidden from God when you were created in the secret place, your mother's womb. He was describing the fact that no one knew you, not even your parents. Have you ever considered that there are places in you that only God knows!!! Places that He can only touch because only He truly knows you. David goes on to explain that He knit you together. Most of us know what knitting is; you start with a ball of yarn and two long flexible rods. Then you begin by wrapping the yarn one rod and transferring it to the other. In the beginning, it only looks like a small chain of loops, however with every unique twist of yarn and the manipulating of the rods you begin to see patterns being formed. If you have ever watched someone knit, it is a tedious, meticulous process. Much work is required before the actual creation is realized. What we see first is an intricate pattern, uniquely created and put together so intensively. Once it is all said and done, you can see the finished product that the designer had in mind from the very beginning. That is the depth in which God knows us even more intimately than someone who has worked to weave the most intricate masterpiece. He knows us. Anyone that would pay such attention to detail has a vested interest in our lives. God never makes a mistake! Do you see His plan forming here, His detailed strategy for your purpose? It is only when we don't know and deeply understand these foundational truths that we are left with feeling unloved, rejected and without focus.

> You were created to RULE!

Your Significance in the Earth

As we continue our journey, we will dig deep into understanding why we are here on earth. God desired that you would be fruitful and multiply, and fill the earth Gen.1:28 KJV. He desired that we fill the earth with creative designs, ingenious inventions to make an impact fulfilling an intended outcome. Fruitfulness is not only procreating, although that is part of it. The word fruitful is explained as "productive, purposeful, creative, and innovative." He then turned the rule and governance of this world over to the human race. We have an opportunity as humans to rule here on earth. There are no other species on the planet that can articulate, design, create, engineer, problem solve or entertain at the level we can. Such is evident in the massive strides we have made in the development of our world. It has always been the plan of God for man to rule in the earth. Genesis 1:26 KJV explains, Then God said, "Let Us make man in Our image, according to Our likeness; and let them rule over the fish of the sea and over the birds of the sky and over the cattle and over all the earth, and over every creeping thing that creeps on the earth."

God created man and gave him dominion over the earth. He was given the autonomy to name every animal on the earth and have rule over them. Gods intention is on display by the fact that He gave us the ability to think and choose, to follow the instinct in us to be who we were designed to be. Wouldn't it be amazing to know that you are doing exactly what you were created to do? Knowing that you are fulfilling an aspect of Gods plan for your life, having the confidence, provision, skills, creativity, wisdom and all things needed to make an impact!!! Have you ever thought about having success guaranteed before you even start a project, simply because that is what you were created to do on earth? You were created to rule! When I say rule, I don't mean as a dictator. I mean that in all that you put hands to do, you are excelling. On your job you are always coming up with creative ideas and solutions, your family calls you blessed because of your understanding in handling the responsibilities of the home In the world, you are sought after as a thought leader because God has given you hidden treasures of wisdom to share. God's plan for your life is that you would become what He created you to be from the beginning of time knowing your identity, fulfilling your destiny, making a significant impact and bringing many to Him.

Change Your Mind!

You are not an accident or a mistake! You may not understand anything about the Bible or even God. However, that does not change the fact that you were created intentionally with destiny on the inside of you. Your life is an intricate pattern created by God to yield a unique tapestry! You can begin to see for yourself that God takes pleasure in you in Psalms 19 and Psalms 104. In Genesis 1 after He created man and woman, the Bible explains, «And God saw everything that He had made and behold, it was very good. Take some time and reflect on what is good about you, not your surroundings, not the jobs you do or the many hats you wear. Focus on you, your personality traits, your character, skills and passions.

Notes

Chapter 2

CHOSEN VS. CREATED

Remember in school when two captains had to pick teams and you hoped that you were chosen early on and not the last one to be selected? I remember holding my breath and on the inside screaming "pick me, pick me!" It feels good to be chosen, it gives a sense of being wanted and approved of, being chosen is good. To be selected as the teacher's helper, a captain of the basketball team, as project lead at work and even to be someone's husband or wife makes us feel accepted. The dictionary defines acceptance as "the action or process of being received as adequate or suitable." The opposite of acceptance is rejection, which means "to dismiss as inadequate, inappropriate or not to one's taste." Rejection is further defined as a failure to show due affection or concern for someone. I am sure that most of us, if not all, can say that we would much rather be accepted than rejected. However, the issue with the reliance on acceptance of people is that it can hinge on so many variables. Individual likes, dislikes, and moods may play a significant factor in whether you will be accepted, even something as simple as whether or not they woke up on the right side of the bed. We can also be rejected because people are insecure, jealous, prejudice and a whole host of other reasons.

A Deeper Understanding

I want to encourage you by letting you know that you were chosen, yes, but you were more than just chosen. You were CREATED by God, specially designed, for a unique purpose. It's a plan that only you have the DNA to fulfill. You don't have to be relegated to an individual's mood or attitude. One day I was thanking God once again for choosing me, saying "God you could have chosen anyone, thank you for choosing me!" His response to me shook my entire being; He said, "I CREATED you for this! The light bulb turned on!!! I was stunned! You mean I was created to be a global world changer, a solution-driven strategic planner, creating good things for the world??!!" By that time, I was more clear about my purpose here on earth which largely had to do with the passion, likes and desires He placed on the inside of me. He created you and me on purpose with a purpose, and it does not depend on whether or not others accept us. This was a total posture shift for me, and it changed the way I saw myself, my relationship with acceptance or the lack thereof and my abilities to accomplish the BIG things the Lord had called me to do. It also took the pressure off me to complete my assignment and placed it back on the One who created me for that purpose. You see, if you know that God created you for an intended purpose, the pressure is on Him to give you the wisdom, the tools, the expertise, the creativity and the provision to complete the task. It's important that we understand that God does not work on a last-minute schedule. He is not haphazard in His planning, nor is he careless or spontaneous. It was His plan all along to create man, the entire universe and to redeem us in such a miraculous way. Please know that you were not a last-minute thought; He didn't say "oh yeah let's make man tomorrow morning." He created a detailed plan, Ephesians 1:4

AMP says, "Just as [in His love] He chose us in Christ [actually selected us for Himself as His own] before the foundation of the world, so that we would be holy [that is, consecrated, set apart for Him, purpose-driven] and blameless in His sight in love."

Even before He created the world, He chose to set us apart for Him with a purpose in view. My close friend and prophetic mentor, Yvonne Camper, author of Healing the Wounds: Prophetic Leadership Transformed, once said to me, "All things prepared!" Those words from the Lord resonated so deeply in my heart because the Lord had been speaking to me about what He had already prepared for me before I was even conceived. The Bible explains, "For we are His workmanship, created in Christ Jesus for good works, which God prepared beforehand, that we should walk in them." Ephesians 2:10, ESV. The New Living Translation gives even greater detail, "For we are God's masterpiece. He has created us anew in Christ Jesus so we can do the good things He planned for us long ago. Ephesians 2:10 NLT.

Let's take the time to unpack this verse. Workmanship is defined by Merriam –Webster as "the art or skill of a workman and the quality imparted to a thing (in this case a person) in the process of making."[2] In the New Living Translation of the Bible, workmanship is referred to as "masterpiece." Essentially, He took His time and designed us so specifically, using His infinite creative skills. He didn't stop there. He imparted in us His nature, His likeness, and as we go deeper, we see that workmanship is from the Greek word, poiema or poem.[3] What a beautiful expression of what we mean to God! As we lay the foundation it is vital that you have the full understanding of who you are and your significance to the Creator. He calls you "His poem, His Masterpiece, His work of art." Once you know, understand and BELIEVE this foundational truth it will shift your mindset and the way you think about who you are. The verse goes on to say that He created us anew in Christ Jesus, we could stop there and spend several days explaining the benefits of being IN Christ. In Christ, we have been made brand new by the sacrifice that He made on the cross. Once we have a clear understanding of who we are IN Christ, we can move in the victory of the cross. He created us for good works ahead of time, preparing the way so that we could accomplish those works on the earth. There are specific things on earth that only you can do, simply because you were predestined to accomplish them.

Change Your Mind!

You are accepted, and by the One who created you! He knew all of the mistakes you would make and all of the insecurities you would have and He still loved you and created you for this earth. Furthermore, He knows better than anyone what gifts He placed inside of you that the world needs. Don't allow the rejection of people keep you hidden from the world. It's time to shine; we need what you have. There is a story about a master that was going away and he gave a portion of talents to his servants. His expectation was that they would use their talents to produce an impact. Each of the servants did something unique with what they had been given. Read Matthew 25:14-30 NIV to find out what each servant did and take some time to ponder on what you have done with the talents you have been give.

Notes

Chapter 3

THE TRUTH ABOUT ME

I should have known that this was all a setup. I had no idea that my life would be full of destiny choices that would lead me on a pre-planned journey out of the mundane to the land of extraordinary. It would have been all too easy just to be born and live a simple life. I had no idea that my life was destined for greatness. Being the only child baffled me for a long time. You see, my mom had several miscarriages, and I was the only child that survived. To intensify matters she almost lost me during her pregnancy. It was difficult growing up as an only child because I longed for siblings. Don't get me wrong; being an only child had its perks, however, I always wondered, "why I survive?" The mere fact that I made it should have given me a clue that my life was extraordinary. At that time I didn't understand that God had a plan for my life, that I was special, unique a thriver, and so much more than that! However, many times throughout my life I felt like I was only surviving, barely making it. Life has a way of tricking you into believing that you are something that you are not; like feeling less than when you are more than a conqueror. The vast majority of us tend to think that we are not valuable. Through a winding path, full of mishaps and disappointments we sometimes end up stumbling down the wrong road, which is what I did. The truth is, our true destiny is often just within reach.

A product of divorce, rejected, abandoned by my father, molested and blamed for it, the list could go on and on and ON, but you get the picture. Rejection seemed to be a reoccurring theme that plagued my life into my adult years. The age-old saying, "if I knew then, what I know now, things would have been different," haunted me for several years, thankfully it is never too late. I pray that throughout our journey together you read something that will turn on the light of your heart, allowing you to realize your actual value. It is far above rubies, and even above the most precious of stones. The things that we value the most here on earth cannot begin to compare to your value to God and your value here on earth.

None of us asked to be here on this earth; we had no choice in who our parents would be, even the circumstances in which we were born were not decided by us and yet here we are. We grew up hearing the voices of our parents; we were thrust into classrooms with strangers, encouraged or discouraged by our teachers, judged by our peers, and governed by our bosses and colleagues. All of that being said we have two choices; we can continue to believe the many voices that have spoken into our lives including our own negative words, or we can seek the truth. What is the truth? The truth is that we were created to be great, do great things here on earth and to have an eternal impact! Each one of us is predestined for greatness. I know you are probably saying, "Yeah, Right!" The problem is, often we don't know what we were created for and our ignorance of that simple but powerful truth conforms us into living life as it comes, accepting situations and circumstances as if they were meant to be. The truth is that before you were born God knew your destiny.

A Leader Foretold

Let's listen in on a conversation that God had with a guy named Jeremiah as He confirmed who Jeremiah was created to be. "Then the word of the Lord came unto me, saying, Before I formed thee in the belly, I knew thee; and before thou camest forth out of the womb I sanctified thee, and I ordained thee a prophet unto the nations. Then said I, Ah, Lord God! Behold, I cannot speak: for I am a child. But the Lord said unto me, Say not, I am a child: for thou shalt go to all that I shall send thee, and whatsoever I command thee thou shalt speak. Be not afraid of their faces: for I am with thee to deliver thee, saith the Lord. Then the Lord put forth his hand and touched my mouth. And the Lord said unto me, Behold, I have put my words in thy mouth." Jeremiah 1:4-9 KJV

The verses we just read explain that there was something in motion even before Jeremiah was in his mother's womb. God created us with an awesome plan and destiny in mind, He set Jeremiah apart, and He gave a heavenly decree that he was to be a prophet. God even set the region in which Jeremiah would preside over. He left nothing to chance, circumstance or fate. He even encouraged Jeremiah when he started with his negative self-talk! Jeremiah wanted to give excuses as to why he could not fulfill his destiny. He was even pre-warned by God that people were not always going to like him, encouraging him not to be afraid of the way people would look at him. I'm sure you are familiar with the phrase "if looks could kill." Sometimes, even the way that others look at us can be quite disturbing. Thankfully, God covered everything that we would ever encounter and gave us many examples in the Bible, just like Jeremiah. Finally, God himself touched Jeremiah's mouth giving him words to speak before he even got to the place where his words would be needed. Now that is amazing! Once Jeremiah had a full understanding of what he was here on this earth to do, he was never the same. There was a paradigm shift that took place in his mind and heart, and he began to walk into what he was called to do.

I decree that you will come into the purpose that God created you for, you will no longer let fate decide or circumstances dictate your life, but you will begin to seek out that which you were placed on this earth to do.

A Royal Mindset

Imagine you were born into a royal family; how would you carry yourself? Would you walk around the palace as a peasant or a beggar? Would you eat out of the trash cans or dress in rags? Of course not! Your mindset would be that of one who has authority; you would be confident, knowing your rights and understanding the Kingdom that you belonged to. You would unapologetically step into your position, knowing that soon you would be King or Queen. Royal families take great care in training up the next heir to the throne. Preparation for your rulership would be inherent. The process would enable you to carry the weight of the kingdom on your shoulders. You would learn what was expected of you from the Royal family, country leaders, and your constituents. You would study the laws and ordinances in order to be effective and efficient in your position. You would surround yourself with wise counsel. Finally, you would be poised to embark on the position in which you trained for your entire life. You may be not in this earth as a king or a queen like in the Victorian age, but you have certainly been placed on this earth to rule, govern, create and lead. Now imagine this in the context of your life. This is the confidence that God intended for us to have in Him.

A Reality of Your Existence

I used to think that I could never speak in front of a large group of people, therefore, I had no clue that I would travel the world and have the opportunity to speak internationally or get married in a foreign country. God has so much in store for you if you allow him to lead you into your purpose. When we align our lives with the plan of the One who created us the reason of our existence begins to come into view. The truth is He knows the thoughts and plans that He thinks toward you plans to prosper you and not to harm you to give you an expected end. (Jeremiah 29:11KJV) Hearing the truth stirs hope on the inside with an understanding that God's plans for you are good. There is a journey that God wants to take you on that leads to a life of fulfillment, growth, joy, challenges, surrender, and impact. It took me a while, but I eventually said yes to the journey and have never looked back.

I grew up in the church and decided that when I got old enough, I would be doing my own thing. I was fed up with "religion," but God still had an awesome plan for me that I could have never dreamed of. Along the way, I was reminded that I am not my own. Let me explain. One day as I was coming home from work in LA with some friends and a car about 200 feet in front of us hit the center divider. My friend put on the brakes at the right moment. Then as the car bounced off the divider and began to come back towards us by another miraculous intervention my friend was able to punch on the gas and the acceleration moved us out of the way just in time to avoid a collision. That was a humbling experience, but not my last brush with death. In the middle of what I would call a BBQ turned gunfight, yes gunfight, my life passed before my eyes. Of course, I was in a place that I should not have been with the wrong people. I found myself running from gunfire.

As I turned to run, I felt a hot breeze on my right ear and then on my left. Yes, two bullets had grazed my ears then went on to hit the leaves of the trees in front of me. I believe I heard this so distinctly so that there would be no mistake in my mind that my life was saved. I am fully convinced that angels guided our car on the freeway and steered the bullets away from my head that day. Realizing at any moment, I could die made me reflect deeply. I asked myself many questions: what have I done with my life? Who knows that I even exist? Is this the only footprint I will leave in this earth? Subsequent events followed, and by the time everything was all said and done, I finally surrendered to God's plan and purpose for my life.

Change Your Mind!

Make a decision today to stop wondering throughout life. You see, making the right choices lead you to purpose. Ask God to show you what He planned for you from the beginning of time and seek His wisdom to walk out your destiny. You are not a peasant, you are ROYALTY! Begin to discover the truth about what God says about those who are IN Christ. Check out these verses Romans 6:6, 1 Peter 2:9 and Ephesians chapter 1, they are great starting points.

Notes

Chapter 4

CO-CREATING WITH GOD

What does it mean to co-create with God? He was the first "creative" and is the ultimate creator, having created this earth, every living creature, the atmosphere, the planets, land and trees, air, ocean and everything in it... there is nothing that exists without God the Creator. He brought it all into existence by His Creative nature. Have you ever taken a moment to think about what He did not create? Rick Jaynor, in his book, Called to Create says," After working six for days, God left the earth largely undeveloped and uncultivated. He created a canvas and then invited us to join him in filling it."[4] How amazing is that?! You are probably saying, "I am not creative at all." Well, I beg to differ. Each of us are creative in our own way. After all God created, there is so much more He left to our imaginations. There were no automobiles, no computers and certainly no Google. It is with this invitation that we can use our gifts and talents to fill this earth with amazing inventions, solutions to global issues and colorful hues that make us smile.

A Peek into the lives of Early Creatives

> Dig deep to pull up what may seem impossible

Ask we discussed earlier, God certainly had a specific purpose in mind for each of us. The story of Noah comes to mind. God gave Noah specific instructions to build what He called an Ark. No one even knew what an Ark was, let alone the fact that the people had never even seen rain. Noah was brave enough to honor and obey Gods request. He co-created with God and developed something that had never been done before. So many others have dared to explore their creative nature to pursue a deep passion, coupled with an innate gift for creating something amazing for the benefit of others. We can also pose the question, "What would we have done without Lewis Lattimer & Thomas Edison's relentless pursuit of the light bulb and the invention of the wheel and the design of the refrigerator from Oliver Evans." Take a moment and ponder this. Have you ever thought that God could have designed you on purpose for a purpose that has not yet been seen or done on the earth! Would you say yes, and respond as Noah did? It's something to consider carefully, God has designed each of us for a unique purpose that will change the course our lives and the lives of others, reshape nations, deliver people from limiting beliefs, save lives, create opportunities and so much more that is virtually unimaginable!

Take a moment to go back to a time in your life when you dreamed or imagined what you wanted to be in life, a time before struggle gripped you, before the trauma and before your innocence was lost. What was it? That dream or desire you had? Dig deep to pull up what may have seemed impossible, what others may have mocked or what may have been buried by fear. Your dream is still there waiting to be fulfilled. Did something come up in your heart? Did you get a glimpse of something once alive in you that no longer is exciting? Take some time and let those thoughts, dreams, and desires come back naturally. You might need to jot some notes down overtime of what you feel as you remember dreams and aspirations that have been dormant. Ask yourself what happened? How did the dream slip away? Is the desire still one that you would like to accomplish? Why or why not? The truth of the matter is that we all have had dreams and plans that have been railroaded by life; however because we were created for a purpose, we can always pick up where we left off.

Nature's Expression of God's Intention

As we continue in our journey, we can see a glimpse of God's intentions as we look at nature. Every animal, insect, and plant has a purpose. The bees pick up pollen and move it from place to place. Pollinators transfer pollen and seeds from one flower to another, fertilizing plants so they can grow and produce food. Cross-pollination helps at least 30 percent of the world's crops and 90 percent of our wild plants to thrive.[5] Without bees to spread seeds, many plants, including food crops would die off. Leaves and sap from the trees can be used for medicinal purposes, the food chain in the ocean from the coral reef, plankton and the Blue whales each serve a unique purpose that He specifically designed. The eco and solar systems were designed all in perfect alignment so that the ocean does not go beyond a certain point on the shore. Everything is in complete order so that we can enjoy night and day, all designed by the perfect Creator!

If He can give purpose to inanimate objects, such as the sun, moon, and insects, how much more to you and I. Our purpose is far greater; He created us with the ability to do great things on earth. Look at Dr. Daniel Hale Williams, who performed the first open heart surgery and Steve Jobs founder of Apple, Inc. Why not you? What have you been Fearfully &Wonderfully Created to do? Have you ever contemplated the fact that your purpose is divinely linked to others? You may be the catalyst for others to do what they were designed to do in this earth. There are certain people that you have been predestined to encourage, partner with, get wisdom from and give wisdom to. Not to mention the communities you are created to develop, hugs you're supposed to give and lives you were created to save. When you begin to follow your passion and purpose, it sparks a chain reaction for others to move into theirs as well. Take a moment to ponder that.

A Life Saved on PURPOSE

In college I had to take a public speaking class, I was terrified. Just a caveat, often the thing you are afraid of is what you are created to flourish in, but we will discuss this later. So, I'm in this class shaking uncontrollably each time I approached the podium to deliver a speech! We were assigned a partner at the beginning of class that we would work with all semester. My partner was an unassuming young man with a scar that went from the bottom of his lip to under his chin. He too was nervous. We worked together for a few months then he said one day, "you may wonder why I have this scar." He went on to say that he had tried to commit suicide, but as he pulled the trigger, the rifle slipped and left him with the scar. I told him that he was still here for a purpose. God did not allow him to die! I continued to pray for him and encourage him the rest of the semester…we are still friends, more than ten years later. I believe that part of my life's journey included meeting and encouraging him. This showed me, in a very real way, that there are so many people hurting in this world for lack of identity and having no sense of purpose. Our lives are made up of billions of small steps that lead us to our destiny. Each day we have the opportunity to walk in purpose; each day we have the chance to make an impact. Some things come quickly, others require intentional focus and hard work to accomplish. I recently had someone to tell me that they believed that they would be guided to their purpose, without seeking it out intentionally. I disagree. Let's be intentional in walking out our destiny.

More often than not, people believe in fate and coincidence which may not lead them specifically to what they were created to do. There is a saying that "the wealthiest place on earth is the cemetery," because of all the unfulfilled destiny's that are there. Let's look at it like this. A butterfly flutters around from one plant to the next there is no rhythm or precise direction to its flight pattern. The butterfly seems to happen on a plant, making twists and turns that are fruitless along the way. Unlike a butterfly, an eagle is precise in its pattern of flight; everything it does has a specific outcome in mind. An eagle's sight is very keen and he is able to see his target, whether it be a destination or prey, a very far way off. There is no point in wandering around in life trying to find what your destiny should be. You have an opportunity to go directly to the One that created you discover your purpose.

Change Your Mind!

This is a significant turning point in your life. Take some time to reflect on past dreams, ideas, business goals, life decisions. What do you feel the most passionate about? What cause or injustice do you want to take up? Are you floating around like a butterfly or moving about like an eagle with a sense of keen focus? What will happen from this point on will depend on you being intentional about seeking the One who created you for your destiny.

Notes

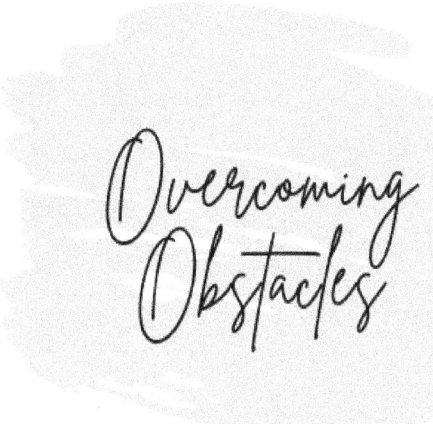

Overcoming Obstacles

Part 2

Since the beginning of time, God has had a plan for our lives. As we laid the Foundation of Truth, we understood that from the beginning we were designed for an amazing purpose. For most of us, there seems to be a huge chasm between the design and the implementation of what God intended us to be. If we are honest, we can identify some of the obstacles that stand in the way, keeping us from being all that we were created to be. In this section we intend to challenge our current perspectives, uncover limiting beliefs so that we can refocus and realign with who we were designed to be from the beginning of time.

Chapter 5

NO LONGER AN ORPHAN

Today may not have been the best time to write about this whole dad issue. However, I have determined that it's an excellent time to capture all of my emotions in the rawest form possible. When you think the dust has settled on an issue, there's a whirlwind waiting to stir up the next storm in your life. Have you ever thought you were over something, and then suddenly the whole thing blows up right in front of you? In this case, I'm the one that did the blowing up. My story, unfortunately, is about my rarely attentive, uninterested dad who filled my life with unnecessary excuses as to why he could not engage in my life or the life of his grandchildren. If you have felt this type of rejection from either of your parents, you can relate to the seemingly unending pain it can cause. I spent such a long time wrestling with feelings of abandonment, rejection, and lies of not being good enough.

If your story is anything like mine and you have had a nonexistent relationship with your father, I hope you find some things on our journey helpful. Where do I even start? My dad has been sporadically in and out of my life, all of my life. The entire scenario was hurtful for me most of my life! My dad left when I was about six year's old. Perhaps even younger; it's all a blur. However, what I do remember so vividly is that every night when my mother and I would drive up to our apartment building; I would lean down in my seat so that I could see high up to our apartment, which was on the fourth floor; I was looking for the light to be on, it never was. I would tell my mom, "I think he is going to be there;" she would say," I don't think so." So many questions flooded my mind. Throughout the years, those nagging questions increased just as the longing deep down in my heart for him to be in my life.

Eventually, he was remarried, and I was, well, an afterthought, at least that is what I felt like. There is no doubt in my mind that the agony and trauma I have faced through the absence and even coldness of my dad has affected my life. I have been married, divorced and now remarried. I chose the wrong mates and missed out on many father-daughter conversations that may have helped me in life choices. Drilling down to the bottom of it all, revealed the brokenness of a little girl that was abandoned and repeatedly rejected throughout the years by her dad.

Introducing My Father

As I stated earlier, I don't pretend to have all of the answers, but I can certainly share what has helped me navigate through these daunting issues. More often than not, when you have faced rejection, the whispering lies of," You are not enough, "or "It's your fault they left," tend to flood your mind and they can overtake you if you allow them to. I have found that a great deal of peace comes from knowing who you are and whose you are. Let me explain. As we discussed earlier in, "The Truth about God", there was a plan set in place for before the beginning of time, and that plan would later include our redemption through Jesus Christ. It is incredible how God already knew that we would experience deep hurts, at times loose our sense of self-worth and even make mistakes in life, so He designed a plan that would cover our mistakes and bring us back to Him. Sin causes separation from God, our creator. When God sent His son into the world to redeem us, there was an exchange that took place. Through His death on the cross, He brought us back to Him, and in exchange, He took our sins and opened the door to a beautiful relationship with Him. It is in this relationship that we begin to understand Father God. You have a heavenly Father that has loved you since the beginning of time. This truth is what has helped me tremendously over the years and even now. Knowing that I have a heavenly Father that loves me with no strings attached, through my failures my fears and my insecurities. This understanding has removed my orphan mentality and I have grown to know that I am not rejected, I am not abandoned but I am well loved and wanted by my heavenly Father.

Unfortunately, you may have had to go through the experience of being an orphan. Many distressful circumstances surround orphans such as abandonment, loneliness, fear of being rejected. Often orphans have no parents living at all or are left with one surviving parent. There are also those that have had both parents in their lives physically, but for whatever reason, they were not good parents. Many times you see this when there is a history of alcohol or drugs. Drug and alcohol addictions as well as abuse play a significant role in childhood traumas. Many of these traumatic events continue from generation to generation which eventually normalizes abnormal behavior in the eyes of the perpetrators. In families where absentee parents exist, nurture, care,

> I had an orphan mentality

protection, and unconditional support is not only lacking but also rare. This can result in individuals who grow up to have difficulty in social relationships, poor behavior and emotional imbalances. Children that grow up in these and similar environments also tend to have an orphan mentality. They often feel rejected, abandoned, unloved and unwanted even though their parents are still alive.

I had an orphan mentality. The trauma of being an orphan can be crippling; specifically, the in area of your emotions, self-esteem, and confidence. Although I was not an orphan physically because both of my parents were living, I had an orphan mentality, and it is important to understand because no one could see me on the inside, no one could help me unless I opened up. I would not open up unless there was someone I could trust. Please understand that trust cannot be obtained unless the environment is SAFE. Many have not had safe environments or safe people in their lives, and unfortunately, the help they need tends to go unnoticed. If you are experiencing trauma find a safe place, a safe person that you can talk with. It is crucial to be able to release what is on the inside of you to someone that will help you, pray for you and many times listen without judgment. If you are reading this and are a safe person, blessings to you! If you feel passionate about helping others, I would take it a step further and get the necessary training so that you can effectively help those around you that need your assistance.

The Role of a Father

When we look at the definition of a father, "a male that gives care and protection for someone or something;" we can see the role that the Father plays in the life of his children and family. Father is also defined as "the first person of the Trinity;

Father God" (dictionary.com)[6] In the Bible the father was of great significance, he was considered the patriarch of the home, city and even the nation. The father had great authority to bless the children. In other words, part of the father's role was to speak words over their children that defined their identity, purpose in life, encouraged them and gave them details about their inheritance. In today's society, the importance of the father's blessing seems to have diminished. Not all parents speak positive, life-giving words over their children. Often it is tough to connect with Father God because of the experiences that we have had with our natural fathers. The author of The Shack, William P. Young, in the Netflix movie, The Heart of A Man, said it took him, "50 years to wipe his father's face off the face of God."[7] Father God is nothing like your natural father, He always has your best interest at heart, He loves you unconditionally, He will never abandon you, and He will never force himself into your life.

In Genesis 27:28-29 Amplified Version we have a clear picture of Isaac pronouncing a blessing over his son Jacob. 28 Now may God give you of the dew of heaven [to water your land], and of the fatness (fertility) of the earth, and an abundance of grain and new wine; 29 May peoples serve you, and nations bow down to you; Be lord and master over your brothers, And may your mother's sons bow down to you. May those who curse you be cursed, and may those who bless you be blessed."

To give you the inside scoop, Esau, Jacob's oldest brother, was careless with his birthright (blessing) and sold it to his brother for a bowl of stew. Isaac, their father, was older and had grown blind when the time had come for the blessing to be given. Jacob went in pretending to be Esau and tricked his father. So, the blessing was given to Jacob, and once the word went out, it could not be revoked. Now, although the blessing Jacob received should have been for Isaac's eldest son Esau, it was still activated in the life of Jacob. Therefore you can see how significant it was. Esau begged his brother to return his birthright to him, but Jacob refused.

Getting in touch with a Good Father

We have a heavenly Father, who has pronounced blessings, destiny and words of encouragement over our lives. Father God is a good father who has made promises that He will keep. He is a protector, the creator of our destiny, peace, and strength. Our Father loved us so much that He gave his son Jesus to take the penalty of our sins (John 3:16 KJV), which brought us near to the Father (Ephesians 2:12-13 KJV). If you have accepted Jesus in your heart, you have been grafted in as a son or daughter of God, able to receive all the blessings of Father God and no longer live life as an orphan. As a child of God, we are free, free from fear and bondage. A good natural father will protect his children, provide for his family, comfort in times of distress and bring peace amid chaos. Romans 8:15, NIV explains, "The Spirit you received does not make you slaves so that you live in fear again; instead, the Spirit you received brought about your adoption to sonship, and by Him, we cry, "Abba, Father." "Abba, Father" is a term of endearment, just as if you were calling your natural father by an affectionate nickname. I encourage you to begin to build your trust in Father God through time spent with Him in prayer, scripture reading, life experiences, and encounters.

I began my journey with the Father reading the Bible only 15 minutes a day, and I was very precise, even using my stopwatch. Guess what? Fifteen minutes daily was just enough to spark my appetite. You know how it is when you read a good book! While you may plan only to read 45 minutes, the next thing you know, that 45 minutes has turned into two hours and you can't put the book down. I became so captivated by the stories in the Bible. It is definitely not lacking in drama, suspense and stories of betrayal & love. Trust me it's all in there!

The Encounter

When my oldest son was born, his father wanted to give him the name Vincent. Although, I had a totally different name in mind, I went along with the name not understanding the depths of God's plan. Once he turned about five years old, I began to hear a little voice whispering to me that he would not live to be ten years old. I know now that it was the voice of the "enemy". At the time I did not have the understanding of who I was in Christ and the "enemy" used that to his advantage to torment me with fear. By the time he was nine years old, full-blown anxiety had taken root. I was praying for him every time he went outside. I had believed, agreed and came into alignment with the enemy's lies. During that time, I attended a Christian conference, and on my return flight home, I was seated next to a woman whose son had passed away at the age of 14. I heard Father God telling me to share the inner torment I had regarding my son. At this point, I had not told anyone, not even my husband. I shared my story with the stranger, and she encouraged me to give the issue to God. What??? How do I do that??? This is my son, and I am supposed to give this to who? I was paralyzed and in a fog. I vaguely heard the stewardess ask, "Are you ok?" In the midst of all that was going on with me internally, we had to de-board our plane because of mechanical issues. I couldn't even

Encounters are unexplained interventions

answer her, as I took my final steps to de-board the plane. What happened next, shook me to the core! "His name means conqueror, His name means conqueror!!!" I knew it was God, and tears began to roll down my cheeks. It was in that very moment that I realized my heavenly Father stepped in and did what I could not do! He was reminding me that the name Vincent meant, "Conqueror"! That told me that everything that comes his way by God's grace, my son will conquer! That day He delivered me from the bondage of fear that my son would die. He knew that I did not have the strength to release it to Him; I didn't even know how. In His love and wisdom, He helped me through the process and from that day forward I never had that fear again, and it's been 20 years! Over the years Father God has continued to reveal new depths of all that He did that day. It's through encounters like this that reveal and reinforce the depths of love that He has for us. In this real-life encounter, He taught me that the blessing that Vincent's natural Father pronounced over him at birth by giving him his name was still in full effect and could not be revoked! If you haven't realized by now, Father God is the one that orchestrated the choosing of the name Vincent. He knew Vincent before I knew him. He knew that his life would be saved and we would learn another layer of who He is! Encounters are unexplained interventions when something greater than yourself is at work to give you courage, strength, hope, and peace during great trials. When encounters take place you know, it had to be God, because everything shifts! Even if we had the best Father in the world, the grace to be a good father only comes from Father God. Our heavenly Father operates on a level far above humanity. Your natural father is human, but not God! You must be able to distinguish and separate the two! In other words your natural father will make mistakes, could be selfish or even abusive, but God does not act or respond in the way that some natural fathers do. He is loving, kind forgiving and so much more.

Change Your Mind!

Father God has pronounced blessings over you! It's time to change your narrative. You are no longer and orphan, you are God's beloved. He knew everything you would ever go through, every mistake you would make, and He still created you. Break out of the orphan mentality and seek out what your REAL Father says about you! Begin taking time to learn about what the bible say about being a child of the King if you have put your faith in God! Starter scriptures include 2 Corinthians 6:18, Romans 8:17, Galatians 3:26 & Galatians 4:7.

Notes

Chapter 6

CRUSHING REJCTION

I have a vibrant yellow shirt that reads "loved." Of course, the shirt when purchased was probably my silent cry screaming out in desire for more love. While wearing the shirt one day, a lady walking by me exclaimed, "That's what I want, to be loved!" I responded, "We all do." Undoubtedly, people all over the world need and want to be loved. However, many do not feel as though they are. No matter how much love they receive, it just isn't enough. Again, we all have a longing within to be loved, accepted and wanted. Though often, love seems elusive. I believe this is the case because we sometimes have a blurred view of what real love is.

It took quite some time for me to get a full understanding of what being truly loved felt like and guess what; it was not what I thought it would be. The wounds of rejection and abandonment had pushed me into developing a false sense of what real love was. I felt if certain things were not done, by those around me, in my mind, it meant that I was not being loved at all. That's what we do when we have not experienced what real love is, often we create our reality which, more often than not, renders unrealistic expectations. Now let me pause here to say that, respect, honor, honesty, loyalty, integrity, and fidelity make up the basic foundation in relationships.

You should expect and offer these pillars in your relationships. If you don't have them in your relationships, your foundation is not sure. You will come across people in which these pillars, in their eyes, are negotiable and they will seek for your love in spite of not honoring these pillars. True love, I mean, real unconditional love can only come from God. He created us and loved us in spite of what we have done, what we look like and what we can or cannot offer Him. No one on earth can love us like He does and expecting that type of fairy tale love from any other human is unrealistic. God created us to be engaged in intimate (close) relationships with Him and one another.

> I felt like no one else knew how to protect me from rejection

There is such a fulfillment that comes from knowing who God is, understanding who you are and developing healthy relationships with Him and others. Unfortunately, at times we are disappointed by people. This can easily cause us to withdraw. Have you been so hurt by people that you have decided to seclude yourself and build walls intended to keep you safe by keeping everyone out? I can relate to this deep introversion all too well. What had seemed like a lifetime of disappointment, hurled me into a prison in which no one could enter! Sometimes you don't even realize that you are locked up. All of your actions and responses come from a place of fear and hurt. I get it! That WAS me. I felt like no one else knew how to protect me from rejection of people better than me. I forgot for a season that I was not my own. I forgot that I had a heavenly Father that loved me beyond measure and sent His son to die for me so that I could be free. Here I was back in a self-inflicted prison as if I was still an orphan with no one to fight for me, protect me or even care for me. I had reverted to an orphan mentality.

If someone had given me this book or even told me that I was going about life in bondage during that time, I would have looked at them as if they were crazy. You may be wondering what happened; how I eventually came out of prison. Well, I took a risk- the risk of trust. I realized that all that time I had shifted from trusting God for His infinite protection to self-protection, and preservation. My way only pushed me deeper into the dungeon of seclusion and darkness where I was constantly tormented. I was depriving myself of the privilege knowing how my heavenly Father would protect me, of knowing what God put on the inside of me and denying others from being blessed by what God had created me to give!

Trust is NOT a Bad Word

The rubber meets the road at our ability to TRUST. Trust is the firm belief of the reliability, truth, ability or strength of someone or something other than you.[7] Let's take a basic example when you go to sit down; you have the firm belief of the reliability and strength of the chair to hold you up. We often put ALL of our trust in people, ourselves or other things in which there is potential to be let down. There is never a guaranteed outcome, therein lies the difficulty of trusting. Trust actually involves you taking a risk. Since we were created for relationship, in life we will need to, at one time or another, put our trust in others. I know that this may be a difficult thing for you to imagine. You may have already felt uncomfortable at the mere thought of having to TRUST someone. I completely understand! It is imperative that you know, I am not saying that you should open yourself up to potentially dangerous people or circumstances. It is best to engage with those that do not verbally or physically attack you, slander your name or gossip about you. We are not doormats for people to walk over. Therefore, in everything seek the wisdom of God about what you share with others as well as asking Him for a strategy to deal with those you have to be in close contact with, such as family members or colleagues that are potentially dangerous. James talked about seeking wisdom and encourages us by saying, "If you lack wisdom, you should ask God, who gives generously to all without finding fault, and it will be given to you." James 1:5 NIV

Building trust does not happen overnight; it takes time and dedication yet can be very rewarding. So how do we navigate through this world with less than perfect people having less than perfect love? In all honesty, I have found that putting my trust in God, gives me confidence, peace AND the courage to engage in relationships with others. Trusting God first provides us with the wisdom in who to consider as close friends, an understanding of ourselves and our role in various relationships. God has given me peace in the relationships that He has led me to engage in and has taught me how to forgive and trust Him to heal me from past hurts. Putting my trust in God to lead me and knowing that He has my best interest at heart, has been very significant in crushing rejection and my response to it in my life.

Our trust in God is crucial and necessary to navigate through life's ups and downs. Trust requires you to put your faith in someone else, and in Gods case, you may not know enough about Him to trust Him. It may also be difficult to trust

Him because you can't see Him. Rest assured He is excited about building a relationship with you. Think of it this way, you can't see the wind, but you know it's there and can have a great impact. It's the same with God. He will have a significant impact on your life for the better if you allow Him to. I encourage you to begin your journey with God, take small steps through prayer and bible study and know that it is possible to have a close relationship with God. Where people may reject you and walk out of your life, you can have the constant assurance that God will never leave you or forsake you. Deuteronomy 31:6 NIV says it so well, "Be strong and courageous. Do not be afraid or terrified because of them for the Lord your God goes with you; he will never leave you nor forsake you."

Jesus' Rejection & Destiny

Another critical component that is helpful when dealing with rejection is knowing your real value. In our world, we rate the significance of an item by its monetary value, the price that was paid for it. Using that same analogy, when Jesus died on the cross to redeem us, His blood was so precious, powerful and concentrated that a single drop could have saved us all. When you know the value of the price that was paid for you, you have a clearer picture of how precious your life is. Your life is priceless; a deeper understanding of this will help strengthen you when rejection comes. Rejection will come! Rejection can take many forms such as jealousy, insecurities of others, divorce, abandonment, abuse, and misunderstandings. Jesus himself was rejected by the very same people that praised Him. The fact that He knew His value and what He was sent on earth to do, allowed Him to stand firm in the face of rejection. Jesus was rejected many times, by His family (John 7:5 KJV), those around Him (Mathew 13:57 KJV) even by those that said they were on his side (John 13:21 KJV). Judas, one of the twelve disciples, betrayed Jesus for thirty pieces of silver. The betrayal took place shortly after Jesus had washed Judas' feet, which was a symbol that Jesus was willing to lay down His life for Judas. We even see that when the time for completion of His assignment on earth had come, God the Father had seemingly left Jesus alone (Matthew 27:46 KJV). He was left alone because Jesus, as part of His assignment, had to take on the sins of the world, to redeem us from the death penalty that sin carried. Let's go to the best teacher, Jesus and observe how He responded when faced with rejection. Luke, recounts what Jesus said in response to those that were crucifying Him. "Father forgive them for they do not know what they are doing." Luke 23:34 NIV

Whew! This is power packed! First of all, Jesus, the son of God, the King of the universe, gave up everything and came down to earth with all humility, putting aside His heavenly deity to fulfill His destiny. His level of surrender to the will of the Father gives us insight into the extreme circumstances He endured to bring forth God's will in the earth. There are no words that can even come close to explain what Jesus sacrificed here on earth. We see two key points in this scripture; Jesus' response to rejection was to forgive and his staunch intentional discipline to fulfill His destiny on earth. We will never have to endure what Jesus did in fulfilling His assignment; however, looking closely at the rejection He faced and endured gives us a glimpse at how important our purpose is here on earth. Let's take a closer look. Jesus knew that He was the King's son, yet He came as a servant. He was clear about His mission on the earth therefore, He was not concerned with being important here on earth. He did not allow the rejection by others to diminish who He was or what He was sent on earth to do. He was intent on moving forward with His assignment. Rejection never changed Jesus' mind about who He was. Many times, we let rejection alter our perception of who we are. Take a moment and think about what comes to mind about yourself during times when you were rejected. He knew that He was the Son of God, no matter what was said to Him or how He was treated. Are you firm in your conviction regarding who you are? Our identity comes from our Creator in heaven. Jesus was obedient unto death, EVEN death on the cross." In Bible times, dying on the cross was the most horrific death a person could suffer. He chose to fulfill His assignment, as grueling as it was. In the face of rejection, pain and death He kept moving toward His purpose. Going back to my earlier point, we can see how His focus was solely on what His purpose was here on earth. Through this, we can now realize that the completion of our purpose here in the earth is vital.

Our Response Determines Our Future

So what do we do? What is our counter-attack, our strategy, our plan of action when rejection comes? Ask yourself right now; what has been my response when faced with rejection? Each of us handles rejection in various ways: do you lash out at the person that rejected you? Remain silent but inwardly seething with rage? Are you crushed internally? Do you sink into depression? Or do you go to the Father for His strength and comfort knowing that He will help you through all that you encounter in your relationships? Each of us has had one, if not ALL, of these responses to rejection at one time or another.

As we observe the rejection in the life of Jesus, we see the pattern that the rejections that took place in His life were distractions designed to keep Him from fulfilling His purpose. His life helps us understand that many of our occasions with

———————
You are
ROYALTY
———————

rejection are meant to detour us from our destiny. One of the effects of rejection is to cause us to view ourselves in a negative and self-sabotaging way. By distorting the view we have of ourselves, we fall for the bait of the enemy and don't see ourselves in the way that we truly are. The enemy uses this tactic quite frequently; we disqualify ourselves in our own minds before we even start on our path toward destiny. That is why it is essential to know that Jesus did not allow the rejection of others to interfere with or to overtake His mind. If we align or agree with the rejection we experience, it becomes very difficult to see the truth of who we are. We will discuss this later in the book when we talk about limiting beliefs. Ultimately, we create barriers that hinder us from moving toward what we were created to do. Think about it. If someone can convince a powerful giant that he is not strong, he won't even go into battle because he is already defeated in his mind. As we discussed earlier knowing the truth about who we are, gives us the right perspective when we are faced with rejection. The truth of who we are can only come from the One who created us, and that truth is our shield against rejection. Remember our example of being a queen. No one can tell you that you are a peasant when you know you are ROYALTY!

Change Your Mind!

It is easier said than done, but please don't take rejection personal. We see that the onslaught of rejection in the life of Jesus was to halt His destiny. What if He gave up due to the rejection of those around Him, even the betrayal that led to His death? Where would you and I be today? Change your mind about what you have faced, what they have said about you, even what the rejection cost you. Instead, shift your focus on your destiny, understanding that what you are going through has been designed to derail your destiny. Change your perspective, and move toward your destiny! I encourage you to take some time to seek out how you will respond the next time you are faced with rejection. Seek God to help you to develop a response strategy!

Notes

Chapter 7

THE BRIDGE CALLED SURRENDER

Have you ever been at a place in life when you realized that you could not trust your own emotions? I remember this season in my life vividly the ongoing pain of disappointment, rejection and betrayal were very tumultuous. I feel like I barreled down as deep as I could go, it began to affect my thoughts, and my emotions were volatile. I was living in total fear and suspicion. My feelings were not to be trusted!!!! Of course, I wouldn't have told anyone else that in an effort to keep it together as much as I could. Many of us have gone through a series of events and diabolical attacks designed to cripple us, even take us out. It doesn't matter your race, status in life or even what's in your bank account. There are circumstances in life that will bring you to your knees, whether you are a Christian or not. We all have a breaking point. Sometimes it is one big issue, other times it may be a reoccurring dilemma or an ongoing barrage of setbacks. Whichever the case, there is a place where the trauma begins to take its toll. My moment was some years ago. The cry for help on the inside of me got louder and louder. It is in these times more than ever that self-care can be lifesaving. It is important that we effectively deal with issues on the inside of us to help bring about emotional wellness.

Matters of the Heart

Let's discuss some common obstacles and strategies to help you to overcome. Let's start by dealing with the matters of the heart, which is very delicate. Let's take a look at the physical heart, if any cell within the heart dies, the entire heart is affected. Emotional distress can be crippling, in fact when you deal with emotional pain, the same message is sent to your brain as if you were in physical pain. Getting the necessary care when dealing with emotional hurt is just as vital as when you are in need of emergency physical care. How do you handle issues that can wreak havoc on your emotions? Maybe the real question should be, "Do you deal with the matters that affect your heart, at all? Many of us push our emotions deep down on the inside without dealing with them. For many women, everything and everyone else takes precedence over their own needs- the kids, husbands, and jobs. So often women come last on their "to do" lists. Ladies, we are important! Realizing that you cannot keep going, taking the hits of life without recovering. We do not have to be superwomen, pretending that we are invincible and that nothing bothers us. Just a side note: I know there are many ideologies today regarding feminism and how women can be like men in everything. I will be the first to stand and say that I am proud to be a woman and do not want to do all a man can do. I agree that there should be gender parity in college graduates, workforce participation, industry sectors well as equal wages for men & women performing the same job duties. However, femininity should not be pushed aside in a quest for a woman to "do and be equal to a man." Your emotional well-being is CRUCIAL!!! A very integral part of maintaining healthy emotional well-being is learning how to protect our hearts. As mentioned earlier, women take on a variety of issues daily, and the things that are closest to our hearts tend to weigh on us. We keep going physically, but often do not deal with the emotional strain that affects us deeply and for some, the guilt of needing help for something that is unseen keeps them from seeking it out. Have you ever been in such anguish and deep pain that seemed to be unending? David said this, "Keep thy heart with all diligence because out of it are the issues of life." (Proverbs 4:23 KJV) Another version says, "Above all else, guard your heart, for everything you do flows from it." Proverbs 4:23 NIV Merriam Webster defines the word diligence as a "steady, earnest and energetic effort."[8] This means we must always guard our hearts with all perseverance and tenacity. One of the ways we can do this is by simply filtering what we let in. When we receive a lot of negativity, it begins to muddy the waters of our heart and pretty soon, we are unable to see things in the right perspective. We do not want our vision to be skewed; we need a clear vision for our destiny! Don't allow yourself to become a dumping ground for gossip, negativity and negative thoughts which we will discuss later.

Dismiss Offenses & Walk in Forgiveness

We can also guard our hearts through forgiveness; this is one of the most important lessons that I have learned. As discussed earlier, rejection will come, but offenses will come also. In Luke 17:1 KJV, He (Jesus) said to His disciples, "Offenses will certainly come, but woe to the one they come through!" We see that we are going to encounter being offended; therefore, how will we respond when it comes? John Bevere, in his book, The Bait of Satan, clearly describes how being offended is the bait that leads us to unforgiveness and encourages his audience not to take the bait! People will do things that hurt us. What is even more difficult is that their actions are enacted upon us with no remorse. Unfortunately, we will encounter people who are very callous and downright mean. There may also be circumstances that may have hurt you deeply: vicious slander from a close friend, betrayal from a spouse whom you trusted, the loss of a loved one, or even abandonment by a parent. These traumatic incidents can undoubtedly bring about offense if we allow them to. However, what we do to guard ourselves against things that may happen to us unexpectedly is essential. Deep within each of us is an innate need for justice. However, when justice is not served, something within us seems to want to hold onto what has happened to us. Let me be the first one to say it is not always easy to forgive, but it can be done!

Forgiveness does not excuse damaging behavior

A fresh perspective on what forgiveness is will help us to release issues and people so that our hearts remain free from bitterness. According to the Greater Good Magazine, "Psychologists generally define forgiveness as a conscious, deliberate decision to release feelings of resentment or vengeance toward a person or group who has harmed you, regardless of whether or not they deserve your forgiveness." [10] Forgiveness is not based on who was right or wrong, whether you did what they accused you of or not, it is not even based on if they apologize. Let me pause here and say that in the past when someone did something hurtful to me, one of the most challenging things for me was to let go of was the lack of remorse and apology from that person! As a child, my mother ingrained that if I did something wrong, it was necessary to APOLOGIZE. Whether they apologize or not, you can still be free from the offense by deciding to forgive. I learned valuable lessons in forgiving others; the most crucial one was the fact that forgiveness was for ME, not the other person! It brought me great healing and much-needed peace when I released others and the negative feelings I had in response to what had been done. I am not a psychologist, by any means yet through my experiences I have learned that forgiveness heals. When you release negative feelings, it melts away anger, brings peace, stops the vexing thoughts of revenge and helps you to move on with your life. Many feel that once they forgive they will be required to be in close relationship with those that have hurt them; this is not true. Forgiveness does not excuse the damaging behavior or force you to forget what has transpired. We cannot control what other people do; however, we can choose, to a certain degree, what effect it has on our lives. Yvonne Camper, author of *Healing the Wounds: Prophetic Leadership Transformed*, says that "When we make other people's behavior about us, we feel victimized, but when it's about them we, ignore it!" Sometimes we need to shift our perspective; this nugget of information was life-changing.

Forgiving oneself is also very vital. Guilt, fear, and shame have a way of overtaking you IF you allow them. I have found that when I do something wrong, repenting and changing my behavior releases me from the guilt of it. There is something about doing the "right thing" that helps the healing process; it also loosens the hold of regret on our lives and helps us to close the door to negative cycles. Forgiveness, whether it be of others or ourselves, requires humility and one the best examples is when Jesus was teaching. Peter asked Jesus, how many times they should forgive. Peter added seven times thinking that forgiving someone seven times was enough. "Jesus answered, I tell you, not seven times, but seventy times seven times!" Matthew 18:22, NLT Forgiveness requires true humility; He was explaining that we have to deny what our flesh wants to do and submit to forgiveness and obedience.

With the help of God, we can walk the humility required to forgive others and bring healing within ourselves.

Control, Duty & Honor Re-Examined

If you are anything like me, you like to handle it all, in the scope of your womanhood, of course. You are a super multitasker and a "get it done" type of girl! From working on projects at your job, to chores around the house and even building your own business, you got this! The mom, wife, CEO, and ministry leader! You are a MASTER Multitasker, as many women are by nature. Just a word of warning, this can turn dangerous fairly quickly if you allow a need for control to set in. Do you feel as if it is mandatory that you take care of every single issue in your life for fear that it will all come crashing down without you? Worry and stress are major blockages to living an emotionally healthy life. These are often a result of trying to maintain control in EVERY area of your life.

Control is a byproduct of self-centeredness and self-absorption. If you have felt closed off to correction, have abused your authority over others, felt the need to tarnish reputations or even criticized others without letting love be your guiding focus, this is an area you need to acknowledge, repent of and seek God's. I know that this may be a tough pill to swallow, but your need for control could be fear in disguise. The danger is intensified when your need to control spills over onto the lives of others. Fear has been described as False Evidence Appearing Real. I like that description because it brings truth to the reality of what fear is. Most of the time fear is fueled by "what if" questions. What if questions have their foundation in the false pretenses that have no basis; their focus is on issues and circumstances that have not even occurred, yet they catapult you into a false reality. In life we cannot effectively control everyone and everything. It is a full-time job that brings forth NO fruit! Honestly, you will never be successful in trying to control everyone and everything. Relinquishing your control over circumstances and people in your life may seem difficult; however, there is peace in letting go. Fear is paralyzing, but surrender brings freedom. You may be asking, "How do I surrender and how do I release everything?" We are often so bound by fear and control that we have no idea how to live in complete surrender. Surrender demonstrates honor, respect, and duty. In Jesus Christ, we witness the ultimate example of surrender. He surrendered His life so that we may be free. I recently read an article by Doug Andre, "What it means to Surrender to God," he shares a fascinating story of a Japanese-born soldier.

"The soldier refused to surrender when the US had taken over the Philippines in World War II in 1945. For 29 years he remained in the jungle, refusing to surrender because he had been ordered by his superiors not to surrender unless he received a specific order that allowed him to do so. Finally, in 1974, the Japanese military sent an officer to give the soldier the order. Branding his military uniform, with his gun fully functional the soldier came out of the jungle to receive the order."

He will not force you to walk in your destiny

Andre, explained that, "sometimes we mix our honor to God with our dedication and honor to ourselves; thus not allowing ourselves fully surrender to God." [11] Often our duty to ourselves, in not surrendering to God, has to do with not wanting to give Him control of every area of our life. So what is complete surrender? Matthew 16:24-25 ESV says, Then

Jesus told his disciples, "If anyone would come after me, let him deny himself and take up his cross and follow me. For whoever would save his life will lose it, but whoever loses his life for my sake will find it." (Matthew 16:24-25, ESV) In losing your life, He means allowing God to lead your life and giving up those things that keep you in imprisoned to fear & control.

What Jesus was saying here is that if you surrender to My will, what I created you to do and be from the beginning of time, you will find your life. Surrender involves yielding your heart, will and plans to that of Gods. It may seem strange to you, because you may have done things your way all of your life. God is the perfect gentleman. Although He created you for a specific purpose, He will not force you to walk in that destiny. That is why it's called surrender because you have the power to choose to relinquish your plans, your will, and your heart to walk in what your REAL purpose, the one that God created you for. In this passage, He also explains that you will have to deny yourself, giving up some of the things you desire to accomplish God's will in your life. I have found that many times what I thought was the perfect plan, the perfect man, the perfect job was not good for me at all, but when I began to trust God and follow His lead things seemed to come together and just felt right. I'm not saying that everything will be perfect in your life; in fact, He asks that we take up our crosses and follow Him. Just as Jesus carried His cross to Calvary and suffered the death on the cross, we too have a cross to bear. There will be things that happen in our lives that are not pleasant; however, the good thing is, that if we have Christ in our lives, we can overcome ANYTHING!

Please know that healing can be a process. If you feel that you need counseling, please seek out someone that you feel comfortable with and that you can trust for your emotional well-being. Remember you are not the only one affected by the trauma you have experienced. Self-awareness is important! Introspection and reflection will save your life AND the lives of those around you. A healthy combination of knowing who you are and your value, forgiveness, having a strong relationship with God and allowing someone to walk alongside you for a season will place you on the road to healing.

Change Your Mind!

Everything we discussed in this chapter requires surrender. Start by making a list of people you may need to forgive, situations that you need to relinquish your control over and circumstances in which you have allowed yourself to be a victim. After some time in prayer begin to, one by one, surrender those issues to God. Release them and be free to move into purpose!

Notes

Chapter 8

Fake ID's

I'm sure you can relate to trying to fit in when you were in high school. It was a time when you were trying to figure out who you were as well as get others to accept you. Some were considered to be class clowns, while others excelled in sports. Some did crazy things to be accepted, and I believe many of us can relate to being something that we should not have, for popularity sake, at one time or another. It was a time when classmates were quick to assign labels such as nerd, loner or teacher's pet. There were also pressures from home as parents compared siblings. Labels have the ability to put tremendous stress on us to perform in certain ways which often forces us to take on identities that were never intended to be part of our original design. You may have known someone in high school that contemplated or even carried out the process of getting a fake ID. In high school, it seemed as if all of us were ready to grow up fast, and for some, a fake id was just the remedy. Essentially the fake ID allowed them to be someone that they were not, gave them access to places they were never supposed to go and in turn, they experienced things that were never meant to experience.

Not everyone has gone through the process of obtaining an actual fake ID. However, a great many carry around fake ID's most of their lives, pulling out the one that fits the immediate circumstance. Whether it is a label formed from your ambitious desires, labels given to you by traumas that you experienced, pressures from parents and peers or just your personal need for acceptance; fake ID's can have a significant impact on your true identity.

I'm not sure about you, but high school was an awkward time for me. Still trying to find my balance and where I fit in, being a "latch-key" kid and not to mention the daily challenges just waking up to face my peers, I unsuccessfully, tried to drown out my inner desire to fit in. I was a good student and quickly found out that I had a knack for basketball. I was moved from junior varsity to Varsity in my Freshman year of high school and seemingly, things were looking up!

> "Rejected" became my most famous Fake ID

However, in what seemed like the blink of an eye, I got hurt and from there things seemed to go downhill. I will never forget the sinking feeling in my stomach as I walked across campus to the portables. "Coach, we need to talk. I'm pregnant." Now entered the label "pregnant teen." I wondered how I even got to that place in high school. How did I feel about myself, my body, why did I give in to the temptations of sex? Part of me was reaching out for love as an orphan hearted kid deprived from the love of my father. It was my senior year, and I was supposed to lead the younger players, however, there I was sitting on the school bus thinking to myself, well, at least someone will love me. I was speaking about my unborn child. I was not confident in who I was created to be, and instead "rejected" became my most famous fake ID. It wasn't until later that I realized how deeply rejected I felt in that moment and in the years that followed. I pressed on with my education as far as I could go until the medical field began to shift to something I was not willing to endure.

"Divorcee" was now the newest label added to my collection of fake ID's. Remarried and two children later I poured everything I had into my family. With the "motha's," meaning the older & supposedly wiser women of the church, telling me that my children were young and that I would have to be a mom for the next 10 to 12 years before I could do something for myself, I felt that my life was for them. Let's stop here for a moment. I want to share with you that it is imperative to seek wise counsel both in and out of the church. When people would ask, "What do you do?" My answer was, I'm a "stay at home mom and wife." I had no further aspirations for the time being because many, (mostly well intending) "church folks" made me feel as though all I was called to do was care for my family for the next decade. Please understand that there is nothing wrong with being a mother or a wife. I want emphasize the fact that if you feel a call on your life to do more, DO IT! In God there is no one or the other, meaning that you don't have to be relegated to either taking care of your children or pursuing your God-given destiny. Seek God and ask Him, what His will is for you in this season and He will lead you.

By now you get my point in regards to how we can quickly amass ID's that don't remotely have anything to do with who we were created to be. Many times we fall into the trap of confusing what we do or what we have been through with our true identity. For example, yes I got pregnant in my teen years, was divorced and was abandoned by my father, but those were only circumstances that I went through, they are not who I am.

True identity comes from the Father, however many of us carry fake ID's. More often than not these fake ID's are the result of what I call fear factors. The fear factors generally stem from the fear of others, the fear of failing, the fear of being rejected, well you get the point. Honestly, at some point in our lives, we have all dealt with one or several of these factors whether trying to fit into society or trying to avoid failure. Unaddressed these factors can become the authoritative voices in our lives, dictating how and when we move forward, respond and go after our dreams or not, how we make decisions and live our lives.

Discovering the REAL You

As I previously mentioned in the opening paragraph of this chapter, fake ID's force you to be someone that you are not, give you access to places that you were not supposed to go and force you to experience things that you were never meant to experience. As a result of fake ID's, you may have found yourself in relationships you should have never been in; relationships that have completely changed the trajectory of your life. Have you seen much more than you should have because you gained access illegally to places you should never have gone? Some have lost years of their lives being in the wrong place, being with the wrong people all because of gaining illegal access to a place they were never meant to be. Take a moment and ponder this. Youth have been sold into slavery, people have overdosed, others have been put in prison for years, all because of gaining illegal access, and experiencing things they should never have experienced.

It is a fact that people such as a verbally abusive parent or a controlling supervisor, tend to place labels on us as well and many times because you don't have a real sense of who you are, you take what others say about you and believe it. The problem is they don't know who you are. It's up to you to peel off the layers of every fake ID that you have carried and every label that was placed on you. Who are you? Have you ever been quiet enough, or sat still long enough to figure out who you are, I mean who God created you to be? From the very beginning, your identity was etched in creation, even before anyone put a label on you. Seek God for your true identity and free yourself from the fake ID's.

Change Your Mind!

So what's in your wallet? It's time to check and destroy every fake ID that you have carried throughout your life! Make a list of all the fake ID's that you identified with and ask God to help you to remove them from your life. Take the next few days to ask God for the truth about who He says you are.

Notes

Chapter 9

WHAT DO YOU BELIEVE?

I am sure that you have heard the term limiting beliefs. Unfortunately, many of us have them. Joyce Meyer coined the phrase "stinking thinking."[12] Before we can ever dream BIG we have to change our minds by getting rid of everything in that is in opposition to the truth, God's Word. The Bible, which is God's Word, is filled with the rich truths about your identity. You may have never read the bible or feel like you can't understand it. A key component of understanding the depths of God's Word is to pray before reading the scriptures. Prayer invites the Holy Spirit to give you clarity and understanding of what you are reading. Let me explain, when Jesus walked this earth God the Father was in heaven. There came a time when He, Jesus', purpose on earth was completed. At that time, He returned to be with His Father in heaven and step into His new role as our intercessor and advocate among so many other roles. At that time, Jesus' disciples were on earth stepping into their assignments and destinies to spread what they had learned from Jesus, around the world. Jesus encouraged them by sending them a helper, He is the Holy Spirit. The Bible explains it clearly, in John 14:26 NASB, "But the Advocate, the Holy Spirit, whom the Father will send in my name, will teach you all things and will remind you of everything I have said to you."

Our Helper

The Holy Spirit was crucial to the disciples as they were charting new territory for the Gospel to be spread globally. It is the same for us today. Navigating through life is difficult, not to mention plowing out our destinies. You may have to chart the new territory of your own business, invent something that no one has ever seen or change current global systems challenging the status quo. This is why God sent the Holy Spirit as a helper, not only for the disciples but to all who have chosen to accept Christ as their personal Savior. The Holy Spirit is vital to the life of the believer. It is also essential for all those that desire to live their lives in a way that is pleasing to God. An amazing bonus is that once you have accepted Christ in Your heart, he promises eternal life in heaven. God's helper, the Holy Spirit can assist you in dealing with life's issues, give you clarity of the scriptures and how they pertain to you in your present circumstances. Here again we see that God gave us a helper, "But when He, the Spirit of truth comes, He will guide you into all truth..." (John 16:13, NLT)

You may be saying, "I have no idea what you are talking about when it comes to the Bible," and I want you to know that it's ok. You may have not yet made to decision to accept Christ in your heart. If you are feeling the tug in your heart to accept Jesus into your heart, you can accept Him by repeating the following prayer:

God, I may not understand everything about you, but I feel that accepting you into my heart is the right thing to do. I repent for the wrong things I have done knowingly and unknowingly. I believe that Jesus took the penalty of my sin on the cross, was buried and rose again bringing me in relationship with you. Help me and teach me about this new journey in Jesus name, amen.

Congratulations, and welcome into the family! For more information about your new salvation, you can check out my website www.reneleawono.com. "Gems from the Kingdom" will give you insight as a new believer.

With your newly found faith, you can now seek the Holy Spirit for a clear understanding of the scriptures and transformation by the truth of His Word. Bill Johnson says this, "I can't afford to have a thought about me in my head that He (God) doesn't have in His head about me. Any time I entertain things that are not true and central in His perspective about me, I'm visiting something that will war against what He thinks about me."[13] This truth blew me away; this was a Selah moment! Let me explain; in the Bible times as readers came across the word Selah they understood that it was a time to take a moment to sit and ponder on what they just read before going on to the next passage. This quote is thought-provoking and explains the necessity of changing our minds before we can move forward into the destiny God called us to. When we have limiting thoughts about our identity, capabilities, and worth it hinders the confidence we need to be who God created us to be. However, as we read and understand the scriptures, they help us to understand the love that the Father has for us, and that all He wants for us is good! Just like a good natural father protects, encourages, affirms and loves their children, our heavenly Father desires the best for us. More often than not, we think much less of ourselves than He does.

> All He wants for us is GOOD!

Now is the time to know what He says about you and to begin to think in like manner.

Dream BIG, But First…

Many of us are very narrow in our thinking, especially as it pertains to capabilities, confidence and self-awareness. Walking out our destinies begins with knowing ourselves, before we begin to dream BIG let's take a look at some practical steps to help us begin to change our thinking. I am intentionally pushing you to pursue another dimension of knowing yourself. This will help you to remove any negative seeds in your life, allowing you to safeguard and nourish the things that will help you to grow from the inside and out. The goal is to become more self-aware, to know and understand your gifts, talents, areas of weakness as well as triggers. Knowing your capacity (ability or power to do) and understanding the way you process information prepares you for inner healing and growth. Additionally, recognizing your tolerance level your (ability or willingness to tolerate behaviors in others that you don't necessarily agree with) also sets you up to rise above any circumstances that you may face. Gaining clarity and self-awareness will assist you in being positioned for success.

There are so many voices that we must compete with nowadays. The voices of society, family members, bosses and co-workers, and even our own inner voice! Honestly, there is only one true voice- the voice of God. What He has to say about you is all that matters! There was a time in my life that I allowed those voices to drown out His truth about me. So, He used another method to get His truth to me. He spoke loudly enough to me through other people that it was undeniable the He was getting a message to me in that season. He began to lead people to speak encouraging words to me, and it got to the point where two or three times a day someone was telling me the same encouraging words and I needed to hear that in that season. I needed to hear that I was stunning, beautiful, valued, wanted, needed, approved of and INDISPENSABLE!!! I knew when it started happening so frequently that God was trying to get my attention, telling me through various ways, that I was precious and highly esteemed. It was now my job to not let those truths slip from my mind but to hold onto them, cherish them and making His truth my truth. This experience transformed the perception I had about myself and helped me to align with the thoughts He thinks toward me.

Many of us have misshaped perceptions in about our identity, ourselves, what people think about, and what we can achieve. We could fill volumes of books with the negative thoughts that try to overtake our minds. What Bill Johnson explains as his mantra is what we also need to focus on. So what do you believe? You may have never asked yourself that question before, or you may be afraid of what is embedded within you. Take courage and begin to ask yourself some difficult questions:

What do I believe about: myself, God, and my abilities?
What do I believe about the Bible?
What do I believe about my future?
Are there any lies that I believe?

When you begin to unveil some of those answers, see if they agree with God's Word. You can do this by praying and asking God, what He thinks about you, you can also read what the scriptures say about you. If you are not familiar with the Bible, a perfect tool is a topical Bible. A topical Bible alphabetically lists where various topics in the Bible and where they can be found. This makes finding out what the bible says, really simple. For example, if you want to look up what the bible says about peace, you find peace in the Topical Bible, and below it, there will be scriptures about peace in the Bible.

Again, when an artist creates a painting or an inventor invents the next new gadget we may not fully understand the purpose of the invention. Therefore, we, go back to the one who created it to get a full understanding of why it was created and what it was created to do. It's the same with us, God created us, and the only way we can have a full understanding of what we were created for is to go back to His words about us. The Bible is His truth and specifically speaks to who we are, what we were created for and our destiny.

Now, Dream BIG

It is time for you to Dream BIG and co-create with God. Great vision, ideas, and plans start in your mind as a thought. If your thoughts are filled with negativity the creativity, solutions to world problems and witty inventions will never break through. Dreaming BIG challenges you to get rid all thoughts, fears, wrong beliefs and shifts you toward what God says about your destiny and you as an individual. It is possible for you to live beyond the limiting beliefs and unrealistic expectations you have placed on yourself. It is possible to rise above those haunting words that they said about you. The Lord shared with me that there are foundational beliefs that gained access into our minds, that are not true and these lies have led to ungodly strongholds. They are blockages that keep us from getting to the next level in God, moving forward in our personal lives, and accomplishing our destinies!

I want to encourage you to DREAM BIG! There are countless ways for you to fulfill your purpose here on earth. When opportunities arise, "Go for It!" As I said earlier often the thing that we are most afraid of is sometimes what God intends to use us greatly in. I used to be afraid of public speaking, and now I have taught classes & workshops, was a spokesperson for an annual "Stop the Violence," rally and have spoken internationally. I want to encourage you to go afraid, go not knowing what to expect, go unqualified as God leads. If you have to, go unprepared and trust God to help you! This may seem unconventional, however, we talk ourselves out of our own destinies for many excuses that come from the self-doubt within us if you aren't sure, which open door is the one for you go in all of them until you know you beyond a shadow of a doubt that this is the one that God has laid out for you. Many miss opportunities and open doors simply because of fear, indecision, and misconceptions. Break free and be all that God created you to be from the beginning of time!!

> Surrender every limiting thought

My prayer is that you surrender every limiting thought and behavior to the Lord and allow Him to be your refuge, comfort, strength, and peace. Allow Him to be your protector and your courage. I remember times when I was so afraid. Situations or people's words would crush me. In those times I would say, "Lord, please protect me, don't allow them to hurt me; guide my words, keep the gates of my lips so that I don't say anything you wouldn't want me to say, help me." He did it every time, and it built up my trust in God. He will protect you throughout the journey to discover your identity in Him as well as pursuing your purpose here on earth. I want to leave you with this scripture as a reminder to help keep your thoughts free from negativity. "And now, dear brothers and sisters, one final thing. Fix your thoughts on what is true, and honorable, and right, and pure, and lovely, and admirable. Think about things that are excellent and worthy of praise." Philippians 4:8 NLT

Change Your Mind!

It is time to Dream Big, but first, you have to clear out all of the stinking thinking that will destroy your progress. Take some time to survey your thoughts… what comes in and out of your mind freely? Do you have a personal alarm that sounds when a negative thought comes in? Are negative thoughts allowed to flow freely in and out of your mental space? If so, begin to evaluate what you are thinking and set boundaries to guard your thoughts.

Notes

Part 3

We are on the road to destiny now, you probably never thought that you would make it! As you begin pursuit of your destiny, there will be some things that you may encounter along your journey. This section will encourage you to step into the extraordinary life awaiting you, with full confidence in God, alert you of some potential roadblocks and awaken your identity. I hope that you are excited today; you have turned the page and begun a new chapter in your life!

Chapter 10

PIECES

When you and I were born, we had no idea what the remaining years of our lives would look like. So, most of us live day by day with the plans and thoughts we have for our own lives; however, as mentioned previously, Jeremiah 29:11 God declares , "For I know the plans that I have for you, plans to prosper you and not to harm you plans to give you hope and an expected end." Jeremiah 29:11KJV.

If you are a planner, you like to have every detail of your life neatly mapped out. Unfortunately, life does not work like that. Most of our lives are like putting together a 5000 piece puzzle, without the box top! It is challenging to see what the finished product will look like when we are connecting the puzzle of our lives one piece at a time. As you begin to uncover clues that point you toward your purpose in life, I want to encourage you to be patient and enjoy the journey. Know that you can rely on the fact that Gods plans for you are to prosper you, not to harm you and that they are set for a specific purpose. It is also important to understand that He has given you the freedom to CHOOSE His will for your lives, which is done through surrender to His will. Your choice to say yes to Him

If money was no object what would you do?

and to what He designed you to be from the beginning of time, gives you full access walk in your true destiny. Take it from my experience; it is so much better to choose the plans of the One that created you, rather than going about living your own way!

Clues to Defining Your Purpose

By now you are probably wondering, so what on earth am I here for? What is my destiny? How do I even begin to figure it out? Well, the truth is that God has already given us hints and clues that we may not have paid much attention to. Those clues are in embedded within your personality and the things you like to do and are passionate about. Are you an encourager? Does it come naturally for you to encourage others? Do you tend to take or be nominated into leadership roles by your peers? Does it excite you to solve problems? Have you always looked out for the underdog or those that are less fortunate? These are questions to ask yourself that may help to lead you to what God intended for your life. What is your dream career? What would you do for free? This would be the thing that would give you the most joy and fulfillment. Finally, if money were no object what would you do?

The bible is full of people being used as great examples, doing great things in the earth. I'm reminded of the story of Moses when he heard from God that he was to be the deliverer of the Israelite nation. He was not confident in his abilities to carry out his purpose. God helped and encouraged him in several ways. God reminded Moses to use what was in his hand (Exodus 4:2 KJV), that may not have been very encouraging to Moses because what he had in his hand was a staff, a simple walking stick! Let's face it. How would you feel going up against a cruel Pharaoh and a massive army with a walking stick? Moses went on to use that stick through God's power to perform many miracles and eventually, by God's instruction he used it for the opening of the Red Sea. The opening of the Red Sea solidified the escape and freedom of the Israelites. There may be something that you have in your hand that is seemingly nothing to you but could be connected to your purpose. It could be an idea, a project, money, a property, the possibilities are endless.

Your destiny may be linked to a specific skill that you have. When Moses was instructed by God to build the Tabernacle, he was given specific details by God. It is no different with you and me; He makes it clear in the following scriptures that He has designed us with detailed plans in mind. In Exodus 31:2-11, NLT, it's explained, 2 "Look, I have specifically chosen Bezalel son of Uri, grandson of Hur, of the tribe of Judah. 3 I have filled him with the Spirit of God, giving him great wisdom, ability, and expertise in all kinds of crafts. 4 He is a master craftsman, expert in working with gold, silver, and bronze. 5 He is skilled in engraving and mounting gemstones and in carving wood. He is a master at every craft! 6 "And I have personally appointed Oholiab son of Ahisamach, of the tribe of Dan, to be his assistant. Moreover, I have given special skill to all the gifted craftsmen so they can make all the things I have commanded you to make: 7 the Tabernacle; the Ark of the Covenant; the Ark's cover—the place of atonement; all the furnishings of the Tabernacle; 8 the table and its utensils; the pure gold lampstand with all its accessories; the incense altar; 9 the altar of burnt offering with all its utensils; the washbasin with its stand; 10 the beautifully stitched garments—the sacred garments for Aaron the priest, and the garments for his sons to wear as they minister as priests; 11 the anointing oil; the fragrant incense for the Holy Place. The craftsmen must make everything as I have commanded you."

In this passage, we see that God gave Oholiab & Bezalel and other skillful artisans the ability to work with their hands to fulfill the purpose in the building of the Tabernacle to a detailed specification. This is evidence that God will prepare you for what you are created to do on this earth. Think about your skills, what you can do with ease. You may be an artist, a singer, an accountant or even a great debater whose destiny is to bring justice by becoming a lawyer! Are you passionate about entrepreneurship? What you are enthusiastic about may be the clue that leads you to your destiny.

The Bible talks about a woman named Lydia, who was a seller of purple. She was a female entrepreneur and converted Christian. In those days it was very challenging to dye cloth, the dyes were natural, and it was very difficult to get enough minerals to dye cloth. In fact, the purple dye was made from liquid found in crustaceans and it took hundreds if not thousands of minerals to create the purple dye. This tells us several things; Lydia was not a poor woman; we understand this because sourcing the items needed for the dye and cloth was very expensive. We also can see that she was a very good businesswoman, selling her expensive cloth at the right prices to receive a return on her investment. The Bible also lets us know that Lydia was from Thyatira, a Roman province in Asia, which was known for the selling of purple. In the book of Acts, we find Lydia was selling her fine goods in Phillipi, which was a region in Macedonia. Lydia took a skill from one region and implanted in another. God may have moved you from one region to another to sell a product or service that would be new to that particular region. While in your hometown, your skill, product or service may have been common, simply shifting to another region will give you the market advantage!

Equally and even more important are gifts that are given by God for the building up of the church inside and out. In Ephesians 4 and I Corinthians 12, I Peter 4 and Romans12 the Bible explains these gifts. God operates through us in many ways to bring His Kingdom on earth. I love what God Word says in James 5:17 NLT, "Elijah was as human as we are, and yet when he prayed earnestly that no rain would fall, none fell for three and a half years!"

> There are no limitations that to what you can do in this earth when you surrender to God!

Elijah had the gift of faith & intercession. What is so radical about this passage is that God intentionally shares this story to let us know that we can accomplish miraculous works too. As humans, we never really believe that we would have any strength over the natural elements, as we see the way God used Elijah in this passage. The truth is we don't have any control over the elements, but Elijah surrendered to God's will and prayed. Obeying God's instructions, Elijah co-labored with God and saw miracles that place. Jesus even said, "Truly, Truly, I say to you, he who believes in Me, the works that I do, he will do also; and greater works than these will he do; because I go to the Father. John 14:12 NASB.

Jesus is saying that we will do the works He did while He was on earth and even greater works. There are no limitations to what you can do in this earth when you surrender your will to God. Do you have a gift of intercession or prayer? Do you have a gift to teach or a heart of deep compassion for people? Your purpose may be to become a pastor, a counselor or an evangelist. God can use you to move heaven and earth.

Who, What, When, Why & Where

Pray and ask God what you were created to do on this earth and who you were created to be? It may be, an encourager, entrepreneur, teacher or an author, or even all of the above! Then ask Him for what people group you are destined to reach? Has he called you to the homeless, the marketplace, to the church, the youth, the imprisoned, pastors, the hungry? Do not forget to ask Him, "what region your sphere of influence is destined to reach. Is it local communities, states or nations?" God gives us clues throughout our lives that point us in the direction of our destiny. Pay attention to what the Lord is saying as you ask these significant questions. Once you feel like you have heard what God has called you to do, WRITE IT DOWN!!! You may not be clear about all the details such as how or when you will accomplish your purpose or even how you will fund it. As previously discussed, most often you will not have the complete vision. Take the time to write down each puzzle piece when you receive it. Habakkuk 2:2 NLT says, "Then the LORD said to me, "Write my answer plainly on tablets, so that a runner can carry the correct message to others." Writing it down is a very crucial step.

I once went to a red carpet awards ceremony for nonprofit organizations. This event was a big deal because no one celebrates nonprofits in this way, at least, none that I know of. The event was designed so that you could freely dialogue with other directors and people of influence. I sat down with a group of influential people, and we each shared what we were doing to help communities locally and abroad. One professional female soccer player, in particular, was very interested in knowing more about my personal involvement with the homeless community I served. She finally, blurted out..." So what do you need, how can I help you!?" Up until that point, I had been feeding the homeless with my own finances, for the previous few years, and had no viable plan of succession beyond that. Needless to say, I was dumbfounded. Without a plan, I lost an excellent opportunity for partnership, funding, and support. I hope you can see the significance of writing down the vision. When you have a plan, you have a guide for others to come alongside through partnerships, collaborations, and prayer. Your plan serves as a blueprint for others to clearly understand your vision. I was listening to an interview between Pastors Steven Furtick and T.D. Jakes, and Pastor Jakes was asked how he accomplished all of the amazing things that he has done in life. Jakes explained that each animal has a defense mechanism and he was curious as to what God gave us. God told him, "I gave you a brain!" [14] We have an amazing opportunity to create with God. Jakes further explained that "God makes trees and it is up to us to make tables, chairs, and furniture! We give up too easily because we don't know how God works. Jakes said that we pray and pray and pray for tables and chairs, and then we get disappointed when He gives us trees!"[15] God desires relationship, and He has so much to share with us, to develop in us and to teach us. Seek Him for the destiny He placed in you from the beginning of time. All things have been prepared for you that you may walk in them.

    I remember the time He showed me an amazing piece of what my destiny would look like. I was overwhelmed but in a good way! Have you ever felt joy, nervousness, and excitement all at the same time! I felt as if I was going to explode, and I couldn't take anymore! Then He softly whispered to me, "What I have shown you is just a screw in the Kauffman Stadium! The Kauffman Stadium is where the Kansas City Chiefs play football. God knows all about you down to every finite detail. I was living in Kansas City, Missouri at the time of this awesome revelation from God about my future. He was saying that all He had just shared with me, which seemed incomprehensible and overwhelming, was just a finite piece of the puzzle in His plan for my life. Just imagine one screw in comparison to an entire football stadium and all the materials it took to build the stadium! I'm sharing this with you to let you know that God has an amazing future already planned for you!

Change Your Mind!

I know it may be tough right now to see the puzzle pieces of your life coming together. I encourage you to take a deep breath, look at the pieces of the puzzle you may have in your hand right now. Can you see this piece fitting into your destiny? If so how? It may be a lesson you are learning. It may be a discovery of something that you are passionate about doing, a person that has the tools, information or skills to propel you to the next steps of your destiny. Take an in-depth look at the pieces you have around you and seek out their meaning. Some pieces you may not understand at this particular time while others will yield an immediate purpose.

Notes

Chapter 11

ORDINARY TO EXTRAORDINARY

When I was a young girl, I was so adventurous and daring. I remember that I was about three years old and I was doing a headstand. My mom was talking on the phone, saw me out of the corner of her eye and quickly ran over to turn me right side up. As I went throughout life it seemed to have gotten the best of me; the cares of life smothered my drive for adventure. How about you? Are there moments from your childhood or other times in your life that seem to be elusive, moments of adventure, courage or even freedom? Guess what, the little girl that was brave, adventurous, joyful, curious is still inside of you. Just for a moment, think about a time before life crashed in, before your innocence was lost and ask God to uncover those virtues in you again

Extraordinary in the Midst of Mess

I'm sharing this with you because I know that God's plans for you are EXTRAORDINARY. He wants you to shift from ordinary vision to EXTRAORDINARY vision! He has always used those that were unassuming to do amazing things. Let's take a peek into some of their lives. David, whom we've mentioned several times throughout our journey, was an adulterer, liar, and murderer. He saw a married woman bathing on the rooftop, desired her and got her pregnant. He then tried to cover it up and sent for her husband to come home from the war, to sleep with his wife but the soldier, Uriah, would not. Uriah was an honorable man and felt that it was not right for him to endure the pleasure of his wife while the rest of his men were fighting in battle (2 Samuel 11:8-17 NKJV). Finally, David's last attempt at a cover-up was to have the army pull back leaving Uriah unprotected during the war. Uriah was killed. David may have hidden his sin from Uriah, but nothing is ever hidden from God. David eventually had to face the consequences of his sin, through the death of his son. From his youth David was destined to be king, at seventeen years old they actually anointed him as the next king. However, during his wait many things took place, some he was not very proud of. The important lesson here is that he was remorseful and repentant for what he had done, God is so gracious and forgiving that He calls David the apple of His eye (Psalms 17:8 NLT). God still used David to do some extraordinary things in this earth in spite of his missteps, and his legacy continues to live on today. I want a positive legacy that lives on for thousands of generations or at minimum until the earth ceases to exist.

> The Lord REMEMBERED her plea

The story of Hannah is a little different than David's, in that she was stricken with barrenness. Hannah could not have a child, which in Bible times was like having a disease, having no children was very humiliating. She was so heartbroken that she remained in the temple praying for a child, till she had no more words. The priest at the time even accused her of being drunk. God, who sees and knows everything, blessed her with three sons and two daughters. She was considered an outcast because she was barren; society would have never looked upon as an extraordinary woman. 1 Samuel 1:19 NLT explains, "The entire family got up early the next morning and went to worship the LORD once more. Then they returned home to Ramah. When Elkanah slept with Hannah, the LORD remembered her plea." What caught my eye as I was reading this story, was the fact that the Lord remembered her. You may not have a barren womb, like Hannah but you may be dealing with barrenness in various areas of your life. Just like Hannah, God wants to fill the womb of your life with good things, fruitfulness. Hannah did not only have one child; she had five children! Her first child, Samuel went on to be a great judge in the bible! God has not forgotten you; in fact, He has specific things planned out for you that you know nothing about! I call these moments, supernatural suddenlies. Supernatural suddenlies are what I define as things that happen in totally unexpected and inexplicable ways. These moments are divine interventions from God, at least that's the way I see it. God always wants to surprise us with a life full of adventure. I want to raise your level of hope and expectation. I understand that you may have been stuck in negative and even barren cycles in your own life, but God wants to increase your faith today and shift you from ordinary to extraordinary.

Your circumstances today DO NOT dictate the rest of your life. I am reminded of a woman at the Jesus met at the well. A Samaritan woman came to the well to draw water at a time when the well was usually free from crowds. The woman had been married five times and the person she was living at that very moment was not her husband (John4:4-42 NIV). At that time racial tensions were high between the Jews and the

Samaritans, and it was forbidden for a single male Jew to be speaking with a Samaritan woman, especially one who had multiple marriages. Jesus was not intimidated by religious leaders of that day, neither was He moved by her current circumstances. He saw and met her need for relationship. The Samaritan woman is mentioned here because you may feel as if you are unworthy to walk into the extraordinary life that God has in store for you. Can I share with you that Jesus went to the well at that time intentionally? You see, no one went to the well at that time because the heat of the day was unbearable, and while the Samaritan woman planned to get her water undetected, God intended to fill her need. Yes, God has a plan for your life, but He also wants to meet your need, so much so that He will intentionally come in right where you are to fill areas of healing, lack, shame, just as He did for the Samaritan woman. He brings you into an extraordinary life, one day at a time.

There were others in the Bible like Rahab, a prostitute that knew nothing about the Christian faith but had heard stories about the God of the Israelites and how He had given victory over their enemies. Rahab had begun to believe those stories, and when Joshua, leader of the Israelites sent spies to scope out her land, she hid and protected them from being captured (Joshua 2 NIV). She and her family were saved as a result of her protection of the spies. Rahab believed the stories about God, and she and her family were saved. God always does something extra special, she was also placed right in the middle of Jesus' lineage, she became a part of the royal bloodline! She ended up being Jesus' great, great, great, well I don't know how many greats, but you get the point grandmother. Rahab was extraordinarily moved from a negative generational background to being in the same family as Jesus.

Many times, we discount the impact our lives have on others or even the potential impact that we can have as we intentionally fulfill our calling. There is so much inside of you that has not yet begun to be realized, I encourage you to move past the obstacles and start to transition into who you have been created to be in this earth! A young girl named Esther had no idea that she would make an impact in her world and beyond but rose to a daunting challenge. She gives us a picture of what it looks like to begin to see your destiny come to past. Esther was an orphan cared for by her uncle Mordecai. When a call came out that the King was looking for a queen, the favor of the Lord was on Esther, and after a long process of purification, Esther was chosen by the King to be his new queen (The Book of Esther, KJV). I have to say that Esther was very young, and she really had no choice in whether or not she desired to be the queen. The royal decree went out and much like a dictatorship... what the King wanted was always granted. Even still the Lord is called the Alpha & Omega, which means the beginning and the end. He knows all the twists and turns that our lives will take even the negative ones we create by our choices. In Esther's life, there was a plan brewing to save a nation, which she knew nothing about. Haman, the King's evil general, demanded that everyone bow down as he rode through the town. The fact that Mordecai, would not bow down and worship Haman, vexed him. Mordecai was a follower of God and would not worship or put anyone before God. Haman was so angry, he devised an evil plot to wipe out all of the Jews! He convinced the King to put out a decree against the Jews that they would be annihilated. Mordecai went to Esther and explained Haman's evil plot against the Jews, and told her this: "For if you keep silent, relief and deliverance will rise for the Jews from another place, but

> Esther's obedience saved her nation

you and your father's house other (relatives) will perish. And who knows whether you have not come to the kingdom for such a time as this?" Esther 4:14 ESV I don't know how you would feel if you were Esther, but I can say that would be like the weight of the world on my shoulders. Here she was an orphan and God had extraordinarily placed Esther in a high position in the Kingdom to save her entire nation! Esther would have to risk her life to get an audience with the King. During that time, it was the custom that when you went before the King, if he did not stretch out the royal scepter to you, you would be instantly killed. Keep in mind that the King had not called for Esther in months, so she was not aware whether or not he wanted to see her. The King received Esther, and she was able through the wisdom of God to unveil the diabolical plan of Haman. The King had Haman, and his entire family killed and issued a decree that the Jews were able to protect themselves against Haman's attack. The Jews prevailed because Esther took a risk and walked in the plan that God had for her life from the beginning of time! You may not be an orphan, but God has a specifically sent you in a job, on a project or assignment for such a time as this. You may know of a particular task that you are to complete that is crucial and will change lives! Her obedience to purpose saved her entire nation, this reminds of Martin Luther King, Jr., Nelson Mandela, Sophia DeBryun and so many others that accepted the challenge to walk into their destinies. Take a moment and look around your life, see what circumstances in which you have been strategically placed to make a difference, bring about change, or even save lives. Will you accept your assignment? It doesn't matter what situation you may find yourself in, God has had an extraordinary plan for your life from the beginning!

> Your life was meant to be filled with extraordinary things

A Peek into My Extraordinary

Growing up as far back as I can remember I always loved Barbie dolls. I had the Corvette, Ken, Barbies boyfriend, the Barbie hotel, clothes and anything else that had to do with Barbie. As most girls do, I dreamed of a wonderful wedding and a marriage full of bliss! None of that prepared me for a divorce and the reality of what my life looked like. Regardless of what things may look like, it does not change what God had in mind for you from the beginning. God has a plan to move you from ordinary to extraordinary, doing some spectacular things along the way! Having gone through all the pain and rejection, I was done, completely finished trying to find who I thought Mr. Right was for me. Little did I know God's plan was just about to kick into full gear! For those that don't know me, I am a hopeful, yes hopeful romantic. I know normally they say hopeless romantic, but I've always been hopeful that God will do something specific in my life. I'm the one who watches those wedding stories like "Say yes to the dress," where the bride and groom fall deeply in love and live happily ever after. I know you may be shaking your head saying that never happens and yes, I thought so too, but I loved the idea of it all.

Did you know that God will give you the desires of your heart? In fact, He places those desires in your heart to bring them to pass especially when you're not expecting it! He did it for me… He unexpectedly brought my husband and me together on a trip, that He unexpectedly paid for, in an entirely different country!!! You're probably wondering where me being a hopeful romantic comes in all of this, well he gave me a romantic fairy tale story that only He could dream up, knowing my heart fully. My husband and I met in Cameroon, yes Cameroon, a country in Africa, spoke only for about five minutes contacted one another via Facebook and planned the wedding six months later in Cameroon with no money! It was adventurous, anointed, miraculous and taught me a lot about how much God loves me so much that he gave me a romantic fairy tale wedding the likes of which I would never have been able to dream up. Now looking back on it I say to myself I would have watched a movie like this, God is in all of the details our lives! He loves planning amazing supernatural surprises just for you!

I share all of this with you to elevate your faith, your life was meant to be full of extraordinary things, places, people and encounters with God! You may have to get rid of bad behaviors and walk through the consequences of them, you may have to pray and ask for a strategy to break out of barrenness. This may even be a season to sever unhealthy relationships that are hindering your purpose. You may even be required to take some risks in God to be catapulted into the extraordinary. Wherever you are at in life, God wants to move you from the ordinary, functioning at a level below what you were created for, to extraordinary, moving in what God intended for you to do and be from the beginning of time!

Change Your Mind!

I believe it's time, your time to rise up. Take one step at a time and begin to live your best life, the life that was designed for you from the beginning of time. Take some time to reflect on your life as it is this moment. Are you fulling your destiny? Is this the legacy you want to leave on this earth? Is there something you have not yet accomplished? Extraordinary is closer than you think…reach for it! Lean all the all way over into God and ask Him about your destiny. I promise He will show you what He had in mind for you, since the beginning.

Notes

Chapter 12

HIDDEN IN PLAIN SIGHT

Have you felt like the world doesn't even notice you? That you have no voice? That you have so much inside of you, yet there is no opportunity to share, no platform, no one even willing to listen? If so, don't be discouraged your destiny is in the making! I used to feel like the 9 to 5 jobs were not for me, and still, do! I was not created to work for someone else. I felt that way not knowing what I was going to do or be on this earth. Guess what, it is alright not to fit the generic societal mold. In fact, I believe it is awesome if you don't fit in! There are times when you know that there is greatness inside of you, but you can't even begin to articulate what it is, not to mention how to pull it out of you. God most certainly knows that He designed you for greatness. However, no one else may seem to notice it! You are not alone. Ecclesiastes 3:1 KJV explains, "To everything, there is a season and a time to every purpose under the heaven."

This essentially explains to us that there is a specific timing for everything, a time in which things are supposed to begin and end. A mother carries her child for nine months, if the child is born before the normal gestation, there could be a significant danger to the child and mother. Science has explained that there are three different stages of development called trimesters, in which significant growth takes place. Each phase of development is critical and focuses on specific organs in the growing baby, at specific times.

There are other examples such as when God created the earth, He created for six days and then rested for the seventh as explained at the opening of this book. He did not continue in creation for thousands of years. As a matter of fact, once He determined that what He had done was good He then gave us the autonomy to create! If you take a moment to ponder the world in which we live virtually everything is governed by time. Our meetings, work schedules, birthdays to name a few. It then begins to make sense that there would be a time for us to begin to outwardly fulfill that which we were designed to do in this earth.

> Much of our hiddenness is actually for preparation

God has a way of keeping you "hidden" to process and prepare you for the purpose He created you for. It makes sense if we consider a growing child; as parents we protect them literally for eighteen years of their lives (sometimes longer) until they are mature enough to live on their own. We teach them life lessons to prepare them for the next phase of life until they go out into the world facing life on their own. This time allows them to go through situations in which they learn amazing lessons in forgiveness, leadership, and integrity which prepares them for future relationships they will encounter and challenges they may face. It is the same for us, in the time of our processing we learn things on the journey that prepare us for where we are going. Often we grow a bit anxious and feel like we are ready when we have no idea what needs to develop on the inside before we are prepared to be thrust out into the destiny that God has planned for us.

Much of our time in hiddenness is actually for preparation, process, and protection. Jesus' ministry was three years; however, the thirty years before the beginning of His ministry was preparation. If Jesus had to prepare for such a long time, we are not exempt from preparation. Jesus was preparing even at the age of twelve years old for what he would not begin until He was thirty years old. However, at the age of twelve, He was separated from His parents, and they had searched for Him for three days. When they finally found Him, He was teaching in the Temple, and His response to his parents was that He must be about His Father's business. (Luke 2:44-49NKJV) It is unclear if Jesus knew at that time all that He would suffer; however, it was evident to Him that He had a specific destiny to fulfill. We see that He was more focused on the will of His Heavenly Father than His will even at a young age. Jesus went on to spend His years touching people, enduring criticism from the religious leaders, bringing to order that which had been in chaos, changing the lives of many, healing the sick and teaching a new and living way. As a man He needed strength to endure all the rejection He faced by the religious leaders that hated His popularity, those that criticized His authority, the many that did not believe in Him, even the one that would betray Him. His journey prepared and strengthened Him for the journey to the cross and agony He would face on the cross.

Seasons of process and preparation can seem frustrating but trust me, God's timing is the best. I didn't always feel this way. I had to mature into wanting God's will more than mine. Now I say, God if I am not ready, please don't put me out there to die! I would rather be processed, prepared, matured and ready in the eyes of God before moving onto the next place of purpose. Some of us behave as teenagers do; always feeling like they want to be out on their own and believe that they know all that it takes to be an adult. The truth of the matter is that they have no idea what is out there waiting to devour them!

The process from the womb to purpose may seem long and tumultuous. Trust me you will need every bit of what you went through, mistakes that you made, the lessons you learned and the wisdom you gained to help you accomplish what you were created to do. To reach the heights that God wants to take you to, you must go deep, and take the time to build a solid foundation. For me, this was illustrated during the demolition of the Wells Fargo building across the street from my previous job. They dug deep into the ground for months until finally, they stopped. It seemed as if they could fit a small city in the chasm! From my vantage point, I could see everything, I watched them build a very detailed network of iron bars before they even poured one ounce of cement down. Level by level they continued to add floors to the building. I understand now that in preparation for the capacity, the height and strength of the building, the depth and intricate details of the iron bars were necessary for a good foundation to sustain the height it would go. On this journey, we have to build properly. Going down deep in God, through surrender, prayer, fasting and reading His Word, allows us to carry the weight of our destiny.

The age-old saying "patience is a virtue," is so crucial. If you have not developed self-control or discipline in God, this season of waiting will be especially difficult for you. When we are hidden in a season of preparation, there will be times that everything within us wants to move forward to fulfill our purpose. Let this be your warning, do not move forward until you know beyond a shadow of a doubt that its time. Time in prayer will yield itself to confirmations from God and open doors which are signals that you are heading in the right direction. As awkward as this seems, rejection at times can also be a signal. I remember there was a season in my life that I found myself with no close friends, I realized later that God would align you with specific people that will help you on your journey; however, everyone is not meant to go with you as you are fulfilling your destiny. Correct alignment is vital, connect with the Holy Spirit and don't take rejection personally even though this is a challenging task! Seek God for His leadership in every area of your life. The Holy Spirit, as mentioned previously, will lead you into all truth. Take your time; promotion comes from God.

Change Your Mind!

Patience is a virtue. Use it! This is not the time to barrel forward, remember you have not been this way before. Never in your life's journey have you been at the place where you are now, wholeheartedly seeking the Lord for your destiny. Each sacrifice and obedient surrender brings you closer to your destiny. Waiting for confirmation to take the next step, may seem ridiculous and even fruitless; nonetheless, I urge you to be patient. You will know when it's time. Acknowledge some times in your life where you moved forward and the timing was not right. As we learn from our mistakes we can see how to navigate the next time around so that we can continue to move forward.

Notes

Chapter 13

ENCOURAGEMENT FOR THE WEARY

There will be times along your journey when it takes all you have to get out of bed, let alone save the world, walk out your purpose or even clean the kitchen! This is normal, Jesus himself was weary at times while fulfilling His purpose. We are human and will experience weariness, sadness, anger and other emotions all along the way. I really believe that Christians often times get caught up in being overly spiritual. Our response to obstacles that come our way is the key to success on our journey. So yes you will, at one time or another, be Fearfully & Wonderfully Created AND tired! The Bible explains to us that, "We have this treasure in earthen vessels, so that the surpassing greatness of the power will be of God and not from ourselves" (2 Corinthians 4:7).

The earthen vessel depicted here is a jar of clay, which if you know anything about pottery, you know that it is very delicate. During the process of making the vessel, the temperature in the kiln when firing it has to be just right, it needs to be handled with care because it cracks very easily. In spite of our fragile, delicate nature, God has placed a treasure within us. This treasure is His power, His strength, authority, compassion, resilience and so much more. There are things that we could not even attempt to do without His precious treasure, for example, we would not be able to forgive or even love one another without His treasure, our helper, the Holy Spirit within us.

Examples of VICTORY

Jesus', when He walked this earth, was fully God and fully man (Hebrews 2:14-18 NIV) yet He needed this treasure to help Him to fulfill His purpose. In fact, the Bible clearly explains that when He went to be baptized by John the Baptist that the dove, descended upon Him. The dove in the Bible represents the Holy Spirit, which is our helper as discussed earlier (Luke 3:22 KJV). During Jesus' journey, he was also tempted on all points (Hebrews 4:15 NIV), yet He was without sin. We see Jesus when he was led to the wilderness and was there fasting (going without food) for 40 days. Satan tempted Him, and he overcame by the Word of God. He had a lot going on throughout His life on earth. On the night before He was to be betrayed and taken to be crucified, He asked that the "cup" of suffering be taken from Him, then said nevertheless, thy will (God's will) be done (Luke 22:42 NIV). He was saying if there is any other way to avoid this suffering, take it away. His is what we often say in our humanness, whenever there are trials and difficulty in our lives. WE WANT OUT! He then said, I still want your will Lord, above mine. Jesus in His journey overcame with obstacles, temptations, and weariness with the Word. This is a lesson for us. We can overcome difficult situations by responding to

> Jesus overcame obstacles, temptations and weariness

them as the Word instructs, gaining strength through the prayer and deep understanding of the Word as well as the use of the Word to destroy the lies of the enemy that come to derail us from our purpose.

In our lives issues will arise that we don't particularly want to face for various reasons. We can look at several other examples of this in the Bible. A man named Elijah had taken on and defeated an evil queen named Jezebel and all of her false gods of Baal. After he prevailed and proved that God was greater than all of the false gods (1 Kings 18:18-40 NKJV), he was threatened by Jezebel and succumbed to fear. He fled from the region and we find Elijah in the wilderness of Beersheba (1 Kings 19:1-8 NKJV) tired, afraid and ready to give up. If you have been facing a string of difficulties back to back, you may be tired! Jezebel and her husband Ahab had been wreaking havoc for years during their reign as king and queen in Israel from c-874 to c-853, she then remained alive until c-843.[16] God's response to Elijah's weariness was to send the angel of the Lord to fortify him with food and to command him to REST (1 Kings 19:5-8 KJV) Often times we take on too much, and we don't take proper care of ourselves emotionally, physically or mentally, as discussed earlier. As we are fulfilling our purpose, we must be very intentional in how we pursue it. Rest, following the leading of the Lord and wisdom are vital keys to success along the way.

There have been times on my journey to fulfilling destiny I myself have been weary, exhausted and emotionally drained. For one, the journey for me has been very long, and there have been times I wanted to give up, times when I felt that all I could do is whisper softly, thank you, Jesus or help me, Jesus. The Bible talks about standing when you have done everything that you could do to stand. At some point you will reach a place that you don't know what else to do, God may even seem silent. The Bible helps us prepare for obstacles that may hinder our journey. Ephesians 6:13 NIV explains, "Therefore put on the full armor of God, so that when the day of evil comes, you may be able to stand your ground, and after you have done everything, to stand."

Standing helps us to maintain the territory that we have already conquered without giving any of that territory to the enemy. Prepare yourself in the word, putting on the whole armor of God and standing firm even amid weariness. When I was on the brink of moving into the place of purpose I had waited years to enter, I had shifted into a stand, I was facing so much all I could do was stand. I was preparing to go out of town on a surprise trip that the Lord had ordained from the beginning of time. God was taking me back to the state where I was born. Unbeknownst to me He wanted to pronounce over me, declaring who He created me to be!. Before I left for the trip, I was mentally and emotionally exhausted. My husband was praying over me, and God spoke to me and said, "Destiny is being fulfilled!" It was amazing. He strengthened me through a tremendous encounter on that trip and encouraged me that the long journey of waiting was over.

Guard Against Overworking

At times weariness can come from us trying to do things in our own way. David was very excited about making sure the presence of the Lord, which dwelt in the Ark of the Covenant, was brought back to Jerusalem. However, David did not consult the Lord or even read the Torah to find out how the transport of the Ark was to take place. His first attempt was what we would call today, an epic fail. Fast forward years later, David attempts again to bring back the Ark this time from

Obed-Edom's house. Obed-Edom knew something that David failed to seek after, in his first attempt to move the Ark. You see, Obed-Edom was a Levite whose family were gatekeepers. They had been given the assignment by God through their leaders to minister in the temple (1 Chronicles 26:6-12 KJV). To explain further, long ago the Levites were set apart in service to the Lord (Exodus 3:5-8 KJV) which meant they had

> Seek the Lord for His direction

the authority to care for the instruments of the Temple, this also is another example of God preparing us for a specific destiny. This explains why Obed-Edom's household was blessed during the time that the Ark of the Covenant was there. (2 Samuel 6:12 NLT) David was not a Levite, and neither were the men he had initially charged with the duty to deliver the Ark; therefore the journey failed. When we try to do things on our own, we get worn out. The Bible explains that the second time David attempted to move the Ark he sought the Lord and learned that only the Levites had the authority to complete the assignment. "No one but the Levites may carry the ark of God, because the LORD chose them to carry the ark of the LORD and to minister before him forever." (1 Chronicles 15:2 NIV)

His second attempt was successful because he followed Gods plan. Such an example shows why it is essential for us to stay in our, own lanes. Many often look at others and try to mimic their successes. You have not been given the grace to walk in another individual's particular purpose; therefore, you set yourself up for failure as David did." It was because you, the Levites, did not bring it up the first time that the LORD our God broke out in anger against us. We did not inquire of him about how to do it in the prescribed way." (1 Chronicles 15:13 NIV)

David brought the Ark of the Covenant on its second journey in accordance with God's instruction, worship, and sacrifice. He had the Levites, the ordained carriers of the Ark, take it to Jerusalem in the proper manner. The distance from Obed-Edom's house to Jerusalem was only 12.5 miles; however, in reverence and adoration to God, David worshiped the Lord and sacrificed animals every six steps!! When you begin to move into purpose seek the Lord for His direction, it will help you avoid wasting time and being worn out by efforts that will eventually be unfruitful. A good friend of mine had a dream about me, and in the dream, there were explicit directions that God was going to give me. There were specific instructions and a warning from the Lord that He had a divine plan and I was to follow His blueprints precisely. Even now I hear a song playing in my ear and it simply says, " I lean not on my own understanding, my life is in your hands you're the maker of heaven!" Will Reagan sings that song with United Pursuit. There is also an excellent version by Leon Timbo. Not leaning on our own understanding is also an instruction given to us by God, in Proverbs 3:5-6 (NLT) "Trust in the Lord with all your heart and lean not on your own understanding; in all your ways submit to him, and he will make your paths straight."

We have an enemy that seeks to disrupt and utterly destroy the plan of God for our lives. The Bible says that "the enemy comes to wear out the saints." (Daniel 7:25 NASB) The Bible also explains our response, "Be alert and of sober mind. Your enemy, the devil, prowls around like a roaring lion looking for someone to devour." (1 Peter 5:8 NIV) I heard it once like this: "The enemy stalks us and looks for points of weakness." I don't know about you, but I am a fighter. When I heard this statement it made me get into my fighting stance; my response was God strengthen EVERY weak place in me! The scripture clearly outlines our response. We are to be alert and sober-minded. Dictionary.com defines being sober-minded as "someone who is sensible and serious."...we are not ignorant of the enemy's devices against us." (2 Corinthians 2:11 KJV) It is our responsibility to do our part to avoid these pitfalls. Remember to check the source when you feel weariness settling in. It may be necessary to change your approach or redirect your response. Part of being sensible is taking rest when needed to avoid being burnt out. As we say yes to the purpose for our lives, we advance in the victory that was already purchased for us on the cross, by using wisdom and following the leading of the Holy Spirit.

Change Your Mind!

When we are weary, we leave ourselves open for mistakes, wrong responses, and indecisiveness. This is not the time to be a lone ranger! Friends you can trust are the best people to have in your life; they will encourage you, share their thoughts and hold you up when you are weak. Also, if they LOVE you will tell you when you are headed for destruction. Take some time and check for areas of your life where you may feel weary or vulnerable ask God to strengthen those areas. Make sure you also put some practical boundaries in place to help avoid weariness. Some of these methods may include, rest, saying "No" to the demands of others and something as simple as planning your day.

Notes

Chapter 14

A RICH INHERITANCE

You have something on the inside of you that was placed there by your creator, God. This is something that the world needs; it may be a book, a service, an entertaining act or a new global system or strategy. In the beginning and throughout your journey you may feel unqualified or even have doubts as to whether or not what you have to offer will be accepted or viable. Trust me you are not the first one to have doubts. In fact, if there were no feelings of uncertainty, I would say that you are not dreaming big enough. Generally, if you can do something without some measure of nervousness or feelings of being in over your head, it's not what you were created to do from the beginning of time. Did you know that you can have a measure of success in life; however, that which you were created for will require a fight to pull out from deep within you? So, what is all this for? Why were you created and why is all of this such a big deal? Why does your purpose even matter?

Let's take a peek into a man named Joshua's life. He was the successor to Moses, who was the deliverer of God's people out of Egypt. After Moses died, it was Joshua's job to take over and lead the people into the promised land. Joshua was a man who was stepping into his purpose, a new destiny. I spent one summer reading through the entire book of Joshua. I read about how God gave Joshua and the children of Israel supernatural victories, such as the fall of the impenetrable wall of Jericho, the surprising defeat their enemies, and finally the takeover and victory into the promised land of Canaan (The Book of Joshua KJV).

A Path of Destiny

As Joshua began his tenure as the leader of the Israelites, I can imagine that he had so many questions. "Will these people follow me like they followed Moses?" "Do I have what it takes to bring us to victory?" "Moses led with a staff; I don't have a staff?" "This first battle seems impossible; will I be disgraced from the beginning?" He was starting a new era. No one had ever done what he was created to do. God in His compassion begins right off in chapter one, admonishing Joshua that no one will be able to stand against him, He encourages Joshua to be strong and very courageous, He promises that as He was with Moses so will He also be with Joshua. He even gives Joshua the end of his the story from the very beginning saying, you WILL lead these people to inherit the land that I promised to their ancestors! (Joshua 1:6 NIV) He further encouraged Joshua several times not to be afraid. God then took away any doubt that the Israelites may have had about Joshua, "And the LORD said to Joshua, "Today I will begin to

> God's promises NEVER fail

exalt you in the eyes of all Israel so they may know that I am with you as I was with Moses." (Joshua 3:7NIV)

The Lord wanted the people to reverence Him and also be assured that He was with Joshua as He was with Moses! The miracle that God performed through Moses, the opening of the Red Sea so that the people would walk across on dry land, was the same miracle that He performed through Joshua at the river of Jericho. Although coming out of Egypt had been a miraculous victory, the fact that the children of Israel had been in captivity by the Egyptians had disgraced their lives. The shame had fallen upon them because of their own disobedience which led to their captivity for 430 years. (Exodus 12:40 NLT) God was so gracious that he called for a time of circumcision. In Bible times circumcision was a token of the covenant man was with God. Today we circumcise our hearts, "cutting away" things that are not of God as a sign that we desire Him above our appetites. After their obedience, God promised that he was rolling away their shame. "Then the LORD said to Joshua, "Today I have rolled away the reproach of Egypt from you." So the place has been called Gilgal to this day. Joshua 5:9, NIV" Joshua went on to defeat Jericho as God miraculously tore down its walls through the acts of radical obedience and miraculous intervention. (Joshua 1-6 NIV).

The book of Joshua is a picture of God's promises that never fail and of His faithfulness. I believe these are the promises that God has for you as you begin your journey fulfilling the destiny that He created for you. You, like Joshua, may have questions, you may not know what to do; you may even be afraid. The children of Israel had to have doubts that this leader would lead them into the promised land because they had wandered in the wilderness for forty years. Just as in the time of Joshua, where a new era had begun, I believe that in your life now, it is time for you to start a new season. It is time for the reproach, the shame that has hung over your life to be rolled away. We see as the children of Israel obeyed the instruction of God and humbled themselves to seek His will, they were successful. I understand that beginning this new journey may seem a bit foreign to you; even impossible at times! You can rest assured that according to Phillipians 4:13 NKJV, you "can do all things through Christ which has strengthened you."

As a result, part of the rich inheritance that awaits you are the never-failing promises of God. Even though the children of Israel were told about the land of promise for generations; but took almost for years to enter in, God NEVER forgot His promises. The book of Joshua and the entire Bible are filled with promises that have been told generations long ago, and God has never and will never forget them. Just as He was with Joshua, He is with you. If you have accepted Him into your heart, you have become an heir to his promises (Romans 8:17a NIV). As we come to the end of the book of Joshua we see that all the promises that God gave to the children of Israel were His gifts to them.

> What you have inside of you is a gift to the world

So the LORD GAVE Israel all the land he had sworn to give their ancestors, and they took possession of it and settled there Joshua 21:43NIV.

The LORD GAVE them rest on every side, just as he had sworn to their ancestors. Not one of their enemies withstood them; the LORD GAVE all their enemies into their hands. Joshua 21:44 NIV

Not one of all the LORD's good promises to Israel failed; everyone was fulfilled." Joshua 21:45 NIV

Giving is the sum of it all. Giving is the reason why Jesus came, it was God who gave His only Son (John 3:16 KJV). God created a leader, Joshua, placing within him the abilities, gifts, and talents needed to lead a nation. Equally important, Joshua said," yes," to his destiny. God then blessed Joshua for doing what he was created to do. He co-labored with God and fulfilled his destiny, and in doing so, many were blessed in the earth.

You were also created to give. What you have on the inside of you is a gift to the world. This is why it is necessary that you pursue what, on earth, you were created to do and be. God has freely given us all things, and it is up to you to intentionally seek out what you were called to do. Do not allow the lie of fate to have you wandering around hoping that your destiny will find you.

The rich inheritance is finding out what was placed in you from the beginning of time, the journey in fulfilling your destiny, encountering the promises of God being fulfilled in your life, leaving this earth full of your legacy and finally enjoying your eternal peace in God.

It is my prayer that after reading this book that you have a better understanding of the importance of your intended purpose and the impact it will have on this earth. Remember, God loves you beyond anything you can imagine, and the proof is the fact He led you to read this book to learn just how much you mean to Him and the world.

"That is why He is the One who mediates a new covenant between God and people so that all who are called can receive the eternal inheritance God has promised them. ..." (Hebrews 9:5 NLT)

Change Your Mind!

Do you have reservations about walking into your purpose? I encourage you to make a list of your doubts, pray and as God for help. Also, take time and write out the pros and cons. At times it may be easier to gain clarity when you can see the issue from a different perspective. God's plan from the beginning was for you to know and understand the rich inheritance you have in Christ, to walk out your purpose and to leave a legacy in the earth. It is now time to GO. DO. BE!

Notes

Notes

1. "The International Standard Bible Encyclopedia." *The International Standard Bible Encyclopedia*, Edited by James Orr, Vol. 1, The Howard Severance Company, 1915, pp. 3104–3104.
2. "Workmanship." Merriam-Webster.com, Merriam-Webster, www.merriam-webster.com/dictionary/workmanship. Accessed 22 Jan. 2019.
3. "Poiema, Greek-Hebrew Definitions." Bible Tools.org, Church of the Great God, https://www.bibletools.org/index.cfm/fuseaction/Lexicon.show/ID/G4161/poiema.htm
4. Jaynor, Rick. Called to Create: A Biblical Invitation to Create, Innovate and Risk. (Baker Books, 2017), 34.
5. Sass, Jennifer. "Bee Facts: Why We Need Bees: Nature's Tiny Workers Put Food on Our Tables." *National Research Defense Council*, National Research Defense Council, Mar. 2011, www.nrdc.org/sites/default/files/bees.pdf.
6. "Father." Dictionary.com, Dictionary.com, www.dictionary.com/browse/father Accessed 22 Jan. 2019
7. " A Heart of A Man." *Eric Esau, Sypher Studios, 2018. Netflix.* https://www.netflix.com/title/80220646
8. *"Diligent." Merriam-Webster.com, Merriam Webster,* https://www.merriam-

webster.com/dictionary/diligent Accessed 22 Jan. 2019

9. "Trust | Definition of Trust in English by Oxford Dictionaries." *Oxford Dictionaries | English*, Oxford Dictionaries, en.oxforddictionaries.com/definition/trust.

10. Carter, Christine. *"What Is Forgiveness?" Greater Good Magazine: Science-Based Evidence for a Meaningful Life*, greatergood.berkeley.edu/topic/forgiveness/definition.

11. *"What It Means to Surrender to God." Unlocking the Bible*, 15 Sept. 2018, unlockingthebible.org/2016/03/what-it-means-to-surrender-to-god/.

12. *Elizabeth. "'Quit Your Stinkin' Thinkin'" (Joyce Meyer)." Beloved Unlovables*, 10 Nov. 2014, belovedunlovables.com/2014/10/12/quit-your-stinkin-thinkin-joyce-meyer/.

13. *Johnson, Bill. "Reigning in Life - Sunday Am." Bethel TV, Bethel TV*, 13 Aug. 2017, www.bethel.tv/watch/4906.

14. *Furtick, S. (2017). How to build your vision from the Ground Up. [video] Available at* https://www.youtube.com/watch?v=aac5si2iKT0 *[Accessed 22 Jan. 2019].*

15. *Furtick, S. (2017). How to build your vision from the Ground Up. [video] Available at* https://www.youtube.com/watch?v=aac5si2iKT0 *[Accessed 22 Jan. 2019].*

16. *Britannica, The Editors of Encyclopaedia. "Jezebel." Encyclopædia Britannica, Encyclopædia Britannica, Inc.*, 22 July 2010, www.britannica.com/biography/Jezebel-queen-of-Israel.

About the Author

Renele Awono is a happily married mother of three, who lives on the West Coast. Psalms 139:14 has been her confession, long before she had the true sense of its meaning. It is her deepest desire to catch up to all God created her to be, daily she walks out this journey one step at a time. If you have not noticed already, Renele is a strong woman of faith, who believes that intentional pursuit of one's purpose is essential.

On her journey, she has obtained her Associates of Arts Degree in Liberal Arts, Bachelor's Degree in Business Administration with a focus on International Business. She has also earned a Minor Degree in Spanish and is studying, the language of love, French. Renele is a humanitarian at heart and throughout her life has sought out opportunities to serve those in need. In addition, she has worked in several industry sectors including nonprofit, local & foreign governments.

In pursuit of her destiny, Renele intends to assist others in seeking out all that they were created to be!

Would you like to more encouragement from
Fearfully & Wonderfully Created?

Check out the website:
www.reneleawono.com

Look out for the upcoming books:
Fearfully & Wonderfully Created Workbook
Fearfully & Wonderfully Created Journal
Fearfully & Wonderfully Created E-books

Check out Social Media:
Instagram: @renele.awono

www.ingramcontent.com/pod-product-compliance
Lightning Source LLC
Chambersburg PA
CBHW062221080426
42734CB00010B/1974